TONI ANZENBERGER · ROBERT ENGELE

GRAZ

EINE STADT IN BILDERN · A CITY IN PICTURES

MIT 208 FARBFOTOS VON
TONI ANZENBERGER

Bildnachweis

Christina Maria Anzenberger-Fink: S. 4 (Foto Toni Anzenberger)
Helmut Lunghammer: S. 4 (Foto Robert Engele)
Steiermärkisches Landesarchiv, Graz: S. 94
Alle übrigen Fotos sind Originalaufnahmen von Toni Anzenberger
All of the other pictures are original photos taken by Toni Anzenberger

Der Fotograf

Toni Anzenberger, geboren 1969 in Wien. Von 1982 bis 1988 Radrennfahrer, Mitglied des österreichischen Nationalteams. Ab 1989 Zusammenarbeit mit der Agentur seiner Schwester Regina Maria Anzenberger. 1990 erste Fotoreportagen, von da an regelmäßige Arbeiten für internationale Zeitungen und Magazine sowie Buchveröffentlichungen und Ausstellungen.
Zum Markenzeichen Toni Anzenbergers wurden die Bildgeschichten um seinen Hund Pecorino.

About the photographer

Toni Anzenberger, born in Vienna in 1969. A racing cyclist from 1982 to 1988 and a member of the Austrian National Team. Has been working together with the agency of his sister, Regina Maria Anzenberger, since 1989. In 1990, first photo reportages, has been working for international newspapers and magazines on a regular basis, book publications and exhibitions since then, Toni Anzenberger's hallmarks are his photo essays featuring his dog Pecorino.

Der Autor

Robert Engele, geboren 1949 in Graz. Studierte Germanistik und Anglistik in Graz und Oxford. Dr. phil. Von 1976 bis 1978 Deutsch-Lektor im Gonville & Caius-College in Cambridge, danach zwei Jahre beim „steirischen herbst" in Graz. Ab 1980 in der Werbeabteilung für einen Grazer Buchverlag tätig, ab 1983 Werbeleiter, ab 1999 Verlagslektor, seit 2003 Journalist bei der „Kleinen Zeitung".

About the author

Robert Engele, born in Graz in 1949. Studied German and English Studies in Graz and Oxford, PhD (1976/78). German lecturer at the Gonville & Caius College in Cambridge, then worked for the "steirischer herbst" in Graz. Began working in the advertising department of a Graz publishing house in 1980, in 1983 advertising director, in 1999 editor, and since 2003 journalist for the "Kleine Zeitung".

Impressum

2. Auflage 2010
ISBN 3-222-13173-2

in der Styria Pichler Verlag GmbH & Co KG, Graz – Wien

Styria Verlag im Internet: www.styriapichler.at

Übersetzung: Andrea Kraus, Graz, und Mark Miscovich, Graz
Umschlaggestaltung: Bruno Wegscheider
Layout: Andrea Malek, malanda-Buchdesign, Graz
Lithografie: pixelstorm, Wien
Druck und Bindung: Druckerei Theiss GmbH, St. Stefan im Lavanttal

Inhalt

7 Die Altstadt – das Weltkulturerbe
8 The Historic City Centre – the World Cultural Heritage

41 Die Stadtkrone – das kaiserliche Graz
42 The Crown of the City – Imperial Graz

57 Der Schloßberg
58 The Schlossberg

69 Die Kulturhauptstadt
70 The Cultural Capital

79 Die Vorstadt
80 The Suburbs

95 Graz im historischen Überblick
96 A Historical Overview of Graz

Die Altstadt – das Weltkulturerbe

Zugegeben – Graz ist eine wirklich faszinierende Stadt mit ihren verträumten Gassen, romantischen Innenhöfen, prächtigen Fassaden, attraktiven Frauen und ausgedehnten Grünanlagen. Wer sich dazu noch in einem der gemütlichen Schanigärten oder Straßencafés – im Sommer ist die Innenstadt nämlich ein einziger Gastgarten – niederlässt, um einen köstlichen Kaffee zu trinken, ist bald völlig dem Charme dieser so südlich wirkenden Altstadt verfallen. Wenn er nicht vorher im berüchtigten Bermuda-Dreieck der Innenstadtlokale um Mehl- und Färberplatz verschwunden ist. Oder sich zwischen den zahlreichen Standln der Bauernmärkte voller Obst, Gemüse, bunter Blumen und scharfer Getränke verloren hat.
Seit 1999 ist Graz Weltkulturerbe wie die Chinesische Mauer oder die Semmeringbahn des Carl Ritter von Ghega. 2003 viel beachtete Europäische Kulturhauptstadt mit neuen architektonischen Akzenten von Kunsthaus bis Murinsel. Dazu seit den späten 60er Jahren beständig heimliche Hauptstadt der deutschsprachigen Literatur, seitdem Peter Handke, Wolfgang Bauer, Gerhard Roth, Werner Schwab sowie Alfred Kolleritschs Forum-Stadtpark-Truppe Bühne und Sprache revolutionierten. Und doch war Graz immer auch Kleinstadt im Grünen und verträumte Pensionopolis der k. u. k. Monarchie. Revolution und Biedermeiertum, unruhige Studentenhochburg und bequeme Insel der Seligen. Gerade diese Gleichzeitigkeit der Möglichkeiten macht die Faszination (und für manche den Frust) der steirischen Landeshauptstadt aus. Denn immer schon lag Graz am Schnittpunkt der Gegensätze ebenso wie der europäischen Kulturen. Und immer schon hat Graz es verstanden, Gegenpole zu vereinen und in neuen Synthesen harmonisch auf-, aber auch untergehen zu lassen.
Die Weichenstellung zur „heimlichen Liebe Österreichs“ (so ein geschickter Werbeslogan der Stadt) mit dem Attribut des Weltkulturerbes fand im Sog der 68er-Studentenrevolte zu Beginn der 70er Jahre statt, als ein Umdenken in Graz einsetzte. Man kam damals von der „autogerechten“ Stadt ab, der zuvor bereits die alte Hauptbrücke und Teile des Kälbernen Viertels zum Opfer gefallen waren. Ein umfassendes Bewusstsein für die historische Altstadt setzte ein, das vom überwältigenden Teil der Bevölkerung getragen wurde. Direkter Anlass war der von Politikerautos ständig verparkte Renaissance-Arkadenhof des Landhauses mitten in der Stadt gewesen, als man hier sogar mit einer Tiefgarage spekulierte. Ein wütender Aufschrei ging durch die Stadt, der sich 1974 in der Aktion „Rettet die Grazer Altstadt“ artikulierte und für den die „Kleine Zeitung“ zum Sprachrohr wurde. Die Erhaltung des historischen Zentrums rückte in den Mittelpunkt des Interesses. Engagierte Politiker, Architekten und Altstadtschützer setzten sich für Fußgängerzonen, Radwege und die Revitalisierung alter Gebäude ein, was am 1. Dezember 1999 mit der Aufnahme der Grazer Altstadt in die UNESCO-Liste des Weltkulturerbes gewürdigt wurde: Eine der besterhaltenen historischen Altstädte Mitteleuropas quillt über von einem harmonischen Architekturmix aus Gotik, Renaissance, Barock, Biedermeier, Historismus, Jugendstil und – als attraktivem Kontrapunkt – spannenden Akzenten zeitgenössischer Baukunst. Vor allem die einzigartig geschlossene und verwinkelt ziegelrote Dachlandschaft des Stadtkerns, die sich schutzsuchend an den mächtigen Schloßberg schmiegt, ist – trotz einiger arger Bausünden – den Aufstieg auf den Schloßberg absolut wert. Der Ausblick entschädigt die Besucher für alle Mühen. Und die stille Abgeschiedenheit der unzähligen Wege durchs tiefe Grün der Bäume und Büsche auf dem Burgberg verschafft dem Besucher unerwartet Ruhe und Entspannung inmitten der Großstadt.

Links: Blick auf die gekrümmte Dachlandschaft der Alten Münze auf dem Schloßbergplatz vom Kriegssteig aus, der 1914–1918 errichtet wurde und steil auf den Schloßberg führt.
Left: View of the curved roof-scape of the Alte Münze on Schlossbergplatz from the Kriegssteig, which is a steep walkway leading up to the Schlossberg that was erected from 1914 to 1918.

The Historic City Centre – the World Cultural Heritage

Granted – Graz is a really fascinating city with its dreamy lanes, romantic inner courtyards, magnificent façades, attractive women, and extensive park facilities. In addition, whoever sits down in one of the cosy pavement or street cafés – actually, in summer, the city centre is one big outdoor dining area – in order to drink a delicious cup of coffee, soon will completely surrender to the charm of the old part of the city with its southern flair. That is, if they haven't already disappeared into the notorious "Bermuda Triangle" of downtown bars lining Mehlplatz and Färberplatz. Or have got lost between the numerous stalls of the farmers' markets, full of fruit, vegetables,

colourful flowers, and strong drinks.
Since 1999, Graz has been a World Cultural Heritage just like the Great Wall of China or the Semmering railway constructed by Carl Ritter von Ghega. In 2003, it received a lot of attention as the European Cultural Capital with new architectural accents from the Kunsthaus (House of Art) to the Murinsel (Island in the Mur). In addition, it has constantly been the secret capital of German literature, since Peter Handke, Wolfgang Bauer, Gerhard Roth, Werner Schwab, as well as Alfred Kolleritsch's "Forum Stadtpark" group revolutionised both the theatre and language in the 1960s. And yet Graz has always been a small city surrounded by nature and a dreamy "Pensionopolis" of the imperial and royal monarchy. Revolution and the influence of Biedermeier life-style, restless student stronghold, and an "island of the blessed". It was just this concurrence of possibilities that created the fascination (and for some, the frustration) of the Styrian capital. For Graz has always been at the intersection of opposites as well as of European cultures. And Graz has always known how to unite opposite poles and to let them harmoniously emerge and sink into new syntheses.
The course for "the secret love of Austria" (according to a clever advertising slogan for the city) together with the attribute of the World Cultural Heritage, was set in the wake of the student revolts of 1968, at the beginning of the 70s, when a process of rethinking started. Back then, the idea of a city "suitable for cars" was abandoned, for which the historical main bridge and parts of the Kälbernes Viertel had already been sacrificed earlier on. A widespread awareness grew for the historic part of the city, which was supported by the majority of the people. The immediate cause were speculations that an underground car park might be built under the Renaissance arcade courtyard of the Landhaus, right in the middle of the city, which was constantly clogged up with the politicians' parked cars. A furious outcry could be heard throughout the city, which was articulated in 1974 in the campaign "Save Graz's historic centre", for which the Kleine Zeitung newspaper was its mouthpiece. The preservation of the historic part of the city became the centre of attention. Committed politicians, architects and defenders of the historic centre, stood up for pedestrian zones, cycle paths, and the revitalisation of old buildings, which UNESCO acknowledged on December 1, 1999 by adding Graz's historic centre to its World Cultural Heritage list: One of Central Europe's best preserved historical city centres overflows with a harmonious architectural mix of Gothic, Renaissance, Baroque, Biedermeier, Historicism, Art Nouveau, and – as an attractive counterpoint – thrilling accents of contemporary architecture. Above all, the unique, continuous red brick roof-scape of the city centre, full of nooks and crannies, which nestles against the mighty Schlossberg as if seeking shelter, definitely rewards one for the ascent to the Schlossberg; despite some serious architectural mistakes. The view from the top makes it worth the effort. And the peaceful seclusion of the countless paths through the rich green of the trees and bushes on the castle hill unexpectedly provides visitors with peace and quiet in the midst of the big city.

Rechts: Das klassische Bildmotiv von Graz – der Blick vom Hauptplatz mit dem Erzherzog-Johann-Denkmal auf den Uhrturm, das Wahrzeichen der Stadt.
Right: The classical picture motif of Graz – view from Hauptplatz with the Archduke Johann memorial up to the city's landmark, the Clock Tower.

GRAWE

Oben: Das Grazer Rathaus gespiegelt: 1888/92 erhielt es beim Umbau des klassizistischen Vorgängerbaus seine späthistoristisch-altdeutsche Zuckerguss-Fassade. Drei der in der Nachkriegszeit verloren gegangenen Nischenfiguren stehen nun wieder auf ihrem angestammten Platz. Die vierte wartet noch auf ihren Sponsor.
Above: Graz city hall reflected: In 1888/92, during the reconstruction of the previous classical building, it received its late historicist, German Renaissance icing façade. Three of the niche figures that were lost in the post-war period are now back in their usual places. The fourth is still waiting for a sponsor.

Rechts: Buntes Spektakel vor dem Rathaus – eine der zahlreichen Aufführungen von Straßenfestivals wie „La Strada" im Sommer.
Right: A colourful spectacle in front of the city hall – one of the numerous street festival performances, such as "La Strada" in summer.

Oben links: Blick über das Erzherzog-Johann-Denkmal auf die alten Häuser im Westen. Ganz links ein mächtiger Renaissanceerker, in der Mitte das große Christophorus-Fresko, das von Franz Ignaz Flurer stammt und 1892 von Paul Scholz erneuert wurde. Eine letzte Erinnerung daran, dass sich hier im 16. Jahrhundert das Gasthaus „Zum hl. Christophorus" befand.
Above left: View past the Archduke Johann memorial up to the old houses in the west. On the far left hand side, there is a mighty Renaissance bay window, and in the middle, one can see the large St. Christopher's fresco, which was painted by Franz Ignaz Flurer and restored by Paul Scholz in 1892. A last memory of the inn, "Zum hl. Christophorus", which was situated here in the 16th century.

Oben rechts: Der Hauptplatz zur Weihnachtszeit – ein buntes Adventdorf mit Lebkuchen, Glühwein und Geschenken sorgt für Stimmung. Die Fassade des Rathauses dient Jahr für Jahr als Projektionsfläche meditativer Lichtspiele.
Above right: The Hauptplatz at Christmas time – a colourful advent village with gingerbread, Glühwein (mulled wine), and presents, creates an enchanting atmosphere. Year after year, the façade of the city hall serves as the projection screen for meditative light shows.

Links: Im Zentrum des Hauptplatzes steht der 1878 errichtete Erzherzog-Johann-Brunnen, der den Steirischen Prinzen umgeben von den allegorischen Darstellungen der vier steirischen Hauptflüsse seiner Zeit zeigt: Mur, Enns, Drau und Save.
Left: In the centre of Hauptplatz, there is the Archduke Johann fountain, which was erected in 1878 and which depicts the Styrian Prince surrounded by the allegorical figures of the main Styrian rivers of that time: Mur, Enns, Drau, and Save.

Links: Erzherzog Johann: Die Liebe zu den Bergen führt ihn 1811 in die Steiermark, wo er das Landesmuseum Joanneum, die Montanistische und die Technische Universität, die Landesbibliothek und das Landesarchiv gründet. Er errichtet Mustergüter für die Bauern und setzt entscheidende Impulse für Bergbau und Industrie.
Left: Archduke Johann: His love for the mountains led him to Styria in 1811, where he founded the Joanneum Provincial Museum, the Mining and Technical University, the Styrian Provincial Library, and the Provincial Archive. He set up model estates for farmers and provided a decisive impetus for mining and industry.

Rechts von oben nach unten: Spätbarocke Madonna mit schwenkbarer Laterne auf dem Kapaunplatz. Das Gemalte Haus in der Herrengasse mit seiner einzigartigen Fresko-Bilderzyklus-Fassade von antiken Götter- und Heldenfiguren, die 1742 vom steirischen Künstler Johann Mayer geschaffen wurde. Ursprünglich war dies der „Herzogshof", denn ehe die Habsburger Mitte des 15. Jahrhunderts eine eigene Residenz in Graz errichteten, wurden die Amtsgeschäfte der Landesfürsten periodisch hier abgewickelt.
Right, from top to bottom: Late-Baroque Madonna with swivelling lantern (Kapaunplatz). The Painted House in Herrengasse with its unique façade depicting a cycle of fresco paintings of classical Gods and heroes, which was created by the Styrian artist Johann Mayer in 1742. Originally, this building was called the "Herzogshof" (Duke's Court), since it served as the venue for the sovereigns to go about their official duties at regular periods before the Habsburgs founded their own residence in Graz in the middle of the 15th century.

Zeit des „Aufsteirerns": Einmal im Jahr wird zur Freude zahlreicher Besucher altes steirisches Volkstum in der Landeshauptstadt lebendig. Da wird steirisch musiziert, getanzt, gesungen und gegessen.
Time for "Aufsteirern": Once a year and to the delight of numerous visitors, old Styrian customs and traditions come alive in the province's capital. Then there is Styrian music, dances, singing, and culinary delicacies.

Sitzungszimmer im Rathaus.
The assembly hall in city hall.

Rechts: Mythologische Figur als Detail des Brunnens im Landhaushof, der eine der bedeutendsten manieristischen Bronzegussarbeiten nördlich Italiens darstellt.
Right: Mythological figure as a detail of the fountain in the Landhaus courtyard, which is one of the most important Mannerist bronze casting works north of Italy.

Rechts außen: Detail des Arkadenganges im Landhaushof.
Far right: Detail of the arcade in the Landhaus courtyard.

Links außen: Die monumentale Eiskrippe des Eiskünstlers Gert J. Hödl, die aus 50 Tonnen kristallklarem Eis als vergängliche Advent-Attraktion im Landhaushof aufgebaut wird.
Far left: The monumental ice crib by the ice artist Gert J. Hödl, which is set up in the Landhaus courtyard as a transient advent attraction and is made out of 50 tons of crystal-clear ice.

Links: Blick durch die offene Galerie des Landhaushofes auf das steirische Wappen, das ein Tor im Landeszeughaus ziert.
Left: A view through the open gallery of the Landhaus courtyard of the Styrian coat of arms that decorates a door in the Provincial Armoury.

Das Landhaus:
Der kunsthistorisch bemerkenswerteste Frührenaissancebau der ganzen Steiermark, ab 1557 nach Plänen von Domenico dell'Aglio als Sitz des Landtages errichtet. Im Vordergrund die offene Galerie, die 1889 zur Abrundung des Renaissancebaus ergänzt wurde.

The Landhaus (House of the Estates):
Seen from an art-historical point of view, it is the most remarkable early Renaissance building in the whole of Styria, which was built as the seat of the provincial parliament according to the plans of Domenico dell'Aglio starting in 1557. In the foreground, there is the open gallery, which was added in 1889 in order to round off the Renaissance building.

In unmittelbarer Nachbarschaft zum Landhaus mit seiner schönen Renaissance-Fassade in der Herrengasse (rechts) befindet sich das Zeughaus, das ab 1642 von Antonio Solar errichtet wurde und als Fassadenschmuck zwei kolossale Nischenfiguren trägt, den Kriegsgott Mars (unten) und die Göttin Minerva (rechte Seite außen).
In the immediate vicinity of the Landhaus with its beautiful Renaissance façade in Herrengasse (right), there is the Provincial Armoury, which was built by Antonio Solar in 1642 and boasts two colossal niche figures that decorate its façade: Mars, the god of war (below), and the goddess Minerva (far right).

Unten: Der gut besuchte Gastgarten im Hof des Zeughauses.
Below: The popular outdoor dining area in the courtyard of the Provincial Armoury.

Oben: Straßenkünstler vor dem Zeughaus in der Herrengasse sorgen für buntes Treiben im Sommer.
Above: Street artists in Herrengasse in front of the Armoury cause quite a colourful ado in summer.

Links und oben: Im Innern des Zeughauses findet sich die größte historische Waffensammlung der Welt. Etwa 32.000 Exponate vom 15. bis zum 19. Jahrhundert – Schwerter, Hellebarden, Helme, Faustfeuerwaffen und Rüstungen – sind in ihrer ursprünglichen Waffenkammer zu besichtigen und zeigen die Bedeutung von Graz im Kampf gegen die Türken.
Left and above: The Armoury houses the world's largest collection of historic weapons. About 32,000 exhibits from the 15th to the 19th century – swords, halberds, helmets, firearms, and armour – can be viewed in their original armoury and show the importance of Graz in the battle against the Turks.

ischer Bau

Links: Blick vom Glockenturm des Landhauses über den barocken Turm der gotischen Stadtpfarrkirche Zum Heiligen Blut in Richtung Süden.
Left: View from the bell tower of the Landhaus over the Baroque tower of the Gothic city parish church "To the Holy Blood" towards the south.

Rechts oben bis unten: Impressionen aus der Herrengasse mit lebendigem Treiben zu allen Jahreszeiten: Gastgärten im Sommer und Adventschmuck zur Weihnachtszeit laden immer zum Bummeln ein.
Right, from top to bottom: Impressions of the bustling and lively Herrengasse all year round: Street-side cafés in summer and advent decoration at Christmas time always invite one to take a stroll.

Oben: Die barocke Mariensäule am Eisernen Tor wurde aus Dankbarkeit für den 1664 errungenen Sieg über die Türken errichtet. Einige Jahre war sie auch nach dem Kulturhauptstadtjahr von einem schlanken Lift begleitet, der den Besucher in Augenhöhe der Madonna brachte – heute steht der Lift in Hartberg.
Above: The Baroque column of Mary at the Eisernes Tor was erected out of gratitude for the victory over the Turks in 1664. Since the Cultural Capital Year, it has been accompanied by a slender lift, which takes visitors up to eye-level with the Madonna. Today you can admire this lift in Hartberg.

Oben: Das Biedermeierzimmer im Stadtmuseum mit einem Hammerflügel von Michael Rosenberger (Wien).
Above: A room in Biedermeier style in the City Museum featuring a piano forte by Michael Rosenberger (Vienna).

Links: Impression aus der Stempfergasse.
Left: Impressions of Stempfergasse.

Das 1905 errichtete Glockenspiel auf dem Glockenspielplatz lockt täglich um 11, 15 und 18 Uhr zahlreiche Touristen zum Verweilen.
Erected in 1905, the chimes on Glockenspielplatz attract flocks of tourists every day at 11 a.m., 3 p.m. and 6 p.m.

Südliche Abendstimmung im „Bermuda-Dreieck“ um Mehl- und Färberplatz, wo schon so mancher Gast verschwunden ist ...
Southern evening atmosphere in the “Bermuda Triangle” around Mehlplatz and Färberplatz, where many a guest has disappeared ...

Blick auf das Café „M 1“ auf dem Färberplatz, das 1989/90 von Richard Ellmer entworfen wurde.
View of the “M 1” café on Färberplatz, which was designed by Richard Ellmer in 1989/90.

Ein kleines Stück weiter führt eine alte „Reiche“ (ganz rechts) wieder zum Hauptplatz zurück. Im Falle eines Brandes bildeten diese schmalen Gassen im Mittelalter eine Barriere gegen das Feuer und boten gleichzeitig (engen) Raum zum Löschen des Brandes.
A little bit further on, an old, narrow alley leads back to Hauptplatz (far right). In the case of fire during the Middle Ages, these narrow alleys provided a barrier against the flames and, at the same time, a (tight) space for putting it out.

Die stimmungsvolle Geschlossenheit der Dachlandschaft aus altem und neuem Ziegelrot mit den vielen barocken Grabendächern und Schopfwalmgiebeln war 1999 mit ein Grund für die Aufnahme der Grazer Altstadt in die UNESCO-Liste des Weltkulturerbes. Ihr gilt auch der ganz besondere Schutz des Grazer Altstadterhaltungsgesetzes.

The impressive uniformity of the roof-scape, made up of old and new red roof-tiles and many Baroque V-shaped and hipped roofs, was one of the reasons why UNESCO added the historic centre of Graz to its World Cultural Heritage list. Its protection is also one of the main aims of the Act for the Preservation of the Historical Centre of Graz.

Links: Franziskanerkirche mit dreischiffigem spätgotischen Langhaus und mächtigem barocken Zwiebelturm. Durch eine kleine Türe in der Klostermauer (Franziskanerplatz 14) gelangt man von außen in den Kreuzgang des anschließenden Franziskanerklosters mit seinen Fresken aus dem späten 16. Jahrhundert, den Sgraffitomalereien und den schönen Epitaphen.
Left: The Franciscan church with its late Gothic nave and two aisles, as well as its mighty Baroque onion tower. Entrance to the cloister of the adjoining Franciscan monastery, with frescos dating back to the 16th century, sgraffito paintings and elaborate epitaphs, is attained through a small door in the monastery's outer wall (Franziskanerplatz 14).

Links Mitte: Die Mur ist in die Stadt zurückgekehrt. Durch die neue Uferpromenade wurde der Zugang zum Fluss wieder möglich – und schon tummeln sich Kanuten und Surfer in den reißenden Fluten.
Centre left: The river Mur has returned to the city. The new riverside promenade once again enables access to the river – and canoeists and surfers are already splashing about in the raging water.

Links unten: 1664 wurde der Turm der Franziskanerkirche murseitig auf kaiserlichen Befehl zum Wehrturm ausgebaut.
Bottom left: In 1664, the tower of the Franciscan church facing the river Mur was built up into a fortified tower by order of the emperor.

Rechts: Stimmungsvoller Blick Richtung Süden. Die auffällige Schrägstellung der Kirche rührt von einem hier früher verlaufenden Seitenarm der Mur.
Right: Impressive view to the south. The church's striking diagonal position comes from a branch of the Mur that once ran along here.

Links: Ecke Schmiedgasse/ Landhausgasse wurde 1882 die Steiermärkische Sparkasse errichtet, die heute den Congress und das Casino beherbergt. Beliebte Ballsäle sind hier der Stephaniensaal und der Kammermusiksaal, die über ein prächtiges Stiegenhaus mit mächtiger Glaskuppel vom Sparkassenplatz aus zu erreichen sind.
Left: The Steiermärkische Sparkasse bank, which today is home to the Congress Convention Centre and the Casino, was built on the corner of Schmiedgasse and Landhausgasse in 1882. Here, the Stephaniensaal and the Kammermusiksaal are popular concert halls and ballrooms. Coming from Sparkassenplatz, they can be reached via a magnificent staircase with a mighty glass cupola.

Von oben nach unten: Blick vom Franziskanerplatz in die Murgasse und zum Paradeishof.
From top to bottom: View from Franziskanerplatz of the Murgasse and the Paradeishof courtyard.

Die Osteria „Don Camillo" beeindruckt nicht nur durch ihre Weine und Speisen, sondern vor allem durch das barocke Gesamtgefüge des Platzes.
People are not only impressed by the wine and dishes of the osteria "Don Camillo", but mainly by the overall Baroque structure of the square.

Ein stimmungsvolles Lokal findet man hier neben dem anderen.
Here, there is one atmospheric bar and restaurant after the other.

Abendlicher Bummel in der Albrechtgasse.
An evening stroll in Albrechtgasse.

Sommerzeit ist in Graz immer auch Festival-Zeit: Live-Konzerte und Filmvorführungen im Landhaushof.
Summer time in Graz is also festival time: live concerts and film screenings in the Landhaus courtyard.

Links: Straßenfestival La Strada: Die niederländische Gruppe Close Act zeigt ihr Stück „Malaja".
Left: La Strada street festival: Close Act, a group from the Netherlands, presents its play "Malaja".

Oben: In den Monaten Juli und August findet in einem Zelt auf dem Mariahilferplatz der Grazer Jazz-Sommer statt, der immer zahlreiche Größen der Szene in die Murmetropole bringt.
Above: In July and August, a big tent on Mariahilferplatz is the venue for the Graz Jazz Summer, which always attracts a lot of outstanding jazz musicians to the "Mur metropolis".

Mitte: Das große Fest des steirischen Brauchtums „Aufsteirern" mit volkstümlichen Weisen und Tänzen auf dem Tummelplatz und auf dem Hauptplatz.
Centre: The great festival of Styrian customs, "Aufsteirern", with popular tunes and dances on Tummelplatz and Hauptplatz.

Unten: Die Gruppe Close Act in voller Aktion (links), der Clown Valentino vor dem Zeughaus erfreut Groß und Klein.
Bottom: The group Close Act in action (left). The clown Valentino entertains both young and old in front of the Armoury.

Das Alte Joanneum in der Raubergasse beherbergt die Abteilungen für Geologie, Mineralogie, Zoologie und Botanik. Das Neue Joanneum auf der anderen Seite des kleinen Parks, der den Rest von Erzherzog Johanns Botanischem Garten darstellt, wurde 1890/94 in der Neutorgasse errichtet. Hier befindet sich die Alte Galerie mit einer großen Sammlung von Kunstwerken aus der Zeit vor 1800.

The Old Joanneum in Raubergasse is home to the Departments of Geology, Mineralogy, Zoology and Botany. The New Joanneum on the other side of the small park, which represents the remains of Archduke Johann's botanical garden, was built in Neutorgasse in 1890/94. It is home to the Alte Galerie (Old Gallery) featuring a large collection of pre-19th century works of art.

Oben: Alte Galerie, Bild „Josef und das Weib Potiphars“ von Johann Carl Loth (etwa 1686), im Vordergrund „Verkündigung an Maria“ von Veit Königer (Detail, etwa 1756). Beide Objekte befinden sich seit Herbst 2005 im Schloss Eggenberg.

Above: Alte Galerie, painting "Joseph and Potiphar's Wife" by Johann Carl Loth (circa 1686), and in the foreground "The Annunciation to Mary" by Veit Königer (detail, circa 1756). Both exhibits have been on display in Eggenberg Palace since autumn 2005.

Mitte: Altes Joanneum, Abteilung für Geologie und Paläontologie, Nachbildung eines Säbelzahntigers, Fundort des Schädelknochens in der Drachenhöhle bei Mixnitz.

Centre: Old Joanneum, Department of Geology and Palaeontology, replica of a sabre-toothed tiger, the cranial bone was found in the Drachenhöhle (dragon's cave) near Mixnitz.

Unten: Direkt daneben ein Megaceros hibernicus oder Irischer Riesenhirsch aus der Eiszeit.

Bottom: Right next to it, there is a giant Irish deer (megaceros hibernicus) stemming from the Ice Age.

Oben: Die neobarocke Schaufassade des repräsentativen Neuen Joanneums in der Neutorgasse mit seinem kuppelgekrönten Haupteingang.
Above: The neo-Baroque decorative façade of the imposing New Joanneum in Neutorgasse. Its main entrance is crowned by a cupola.

Unten: Blick auf den St. Lambrechter Hof in der Raubergasse. Der hier sichtbare nördliche Teil des Gebäudes wurde 1665/74 im Auftrag des obersteirischen Klosters St. Lambrecht erbaut. Der südliche Teil ab der Traufe wurde Anfang des 19. Jahrhunderts errichtet und der barocken Fassade angepasst. Hier ist das Alte Joanneum untergebracht.
Bottom: View of the St. Lambrechter Hof building on Raubergasse. In 1665/74, the Upper-Styrian monastery of St. Lambrecht commissioned the construction of the northern part of the building which is visible in the picture. The southern part, starting from the eaves, was built in the 19th century and was adapted to the Baroque façade. It is home to the Old Joanneum.

Die Grazer Oper wurde 1898/99 nach den Plänen der beiden Wiener Theaterarchitekten Ferdinand Fellner und Eduard Helmer erbaut. 1944 erlitt das Gebäude einen Bombentreffer, als dessen Ergebnis nun ein Terrassenvorbau die nördliche Fassade zum Opernring schmückt.

The opera of Graz was built in 1898/99 according to the plans of the two Viennese theatre architects, Ferdinand Fellner and Eduard Helmer. In 1944, the building suffered a direct bomb hit which destroyed the top part of the original portico. A large balcony was built on top of the remaining part and integrated into the northern facade facing the Opernring.

Links: Das Innere im Stil eines klassischen Logen- und Rangtheaters ist in üppiger Rokokodekoration prunkvoll ausgestattet und bietet Platz für 1500 Sitze, 48 Logen und vier Repräsentationslogen.
Left: The interior, in the style of a classical box and rank theatre, is furnished in the most luxurious Rococo decoration and seats 1,500 people, with 48 normal and 4 representative loges.

Rechts: Die 54 Meter hohe Skulptur „Lichtschwert" des steirischen Künstlers Hartmut Skerbisch gibt in Originalgröße die Innenkonstruktion der New Yorker Freiheitsstatue wieder und wurde im Rahmen des steirischen herbstes 1992 zur 500-Jahr-Feier der Entdeckung Amerikas direkt neben dem Opernhaus aufgestellt.
Right: The 54-metre tall "Lichtschwert" (light sword) sculpture by the Styrian artist Hartmut Skerbisch resembles the full-scale internal structure of New York's Statue of Liberty. It was put up right next to the opera house as part of the steirischer herbst 1992 on the occasion of the 500th anniversary of the discovery of America.

Rechts unten: Bauernmarkt auf dem Kaiser-Josef-Platz. Hier biegen sich die Verkaufstische unter der Buntheit steirischer Früchte und Gemüsesorten – Kernöl, geselchtes Fleisch, Brot und die verschiedensten Sorten von farbenfrohen Blumen und Pflanzen nicht zu vergessen.
Bottom right: Farmers' market on Kaiser-Josef-Platz. Here, the tables sag under the diversity of Styrian fruit and vegetables – not to mention the pumpkin seed oil, smoked meat, bread and the most varied kinds of colourful flowers and plants.

Täglich etwa 100.000 Menschen frequentieren den Jakominiplatz, haben Zählungen ergeben. Kein Wunder, ist er doch Drehscheibe des gesamten öffentlichen Verkehrs in Graz. 1996 erfolgte die umstrittene Neugestaltung durch die Grazer Architekten Jörg und Ingrid Mayr, die mit zahllosen Leuchtmasten und viel Buntheit die Bedeutung als öffentlicher Raum betonen wollten.

About 100,000 people frequent Jakominiplatz a day, according to recent counts. No wonder, since the square is the hub of all of Graz' public transportation. In 1996, the architect couple Jörg and Ingrid Mayr set about the controversial complete redesigning of the square. They wanted to emphasise its importance as a public space by means of numerous light poles and a lot of colour.

Oben: Florale Jugendstilfassade des Hauses Sporgasse 3, dessen Stuckdekoration vom Bildhauer Georg Winkler stammt.
Above: The floral Art Nouveau façade of the house at Sporgasse No. 3, whose stucco decoration was created by the sculptor Georg Winkler.

Unten: Innenhof der Neuen Galerie mit „Blase in die Ecke“ von Hans Kupelwieser (Sommer 2004), dessen Betonguss-Erdäpfel „Patatas“ als Erinnerung an Graz 2003 im Augarten auf grüner Wiese zu sehen sind.
Bottom: Inner courtyard of the New Gallery with “Bubble in the Corner” by Hans Kupelwieser (summer 2004), whose cast concrete potatoes “Patatas” can be seen on the green lawn of the Augarten park in commemoration of Graz 2003.

Rechts: Repräsentatives Treppenhaus im Palais Herberstein, 1754/57 von Josef Hueber errichtet, heute Neue Galerie.
Right: Representative staircase built by Josef Hueber in 1754/57, in Palais Herberstein, today's New Gallery.

Ein Hauch von südlicher Atmosphäre liegt über den Straßenlokalen an der Ecke Sporgasse/Hauptplatz neben den spätgotischen Laubengängen des Luegg-Hauses (rechts und unten rechts).
A slight touch of Southern flair hovers over the bars and restaurants on the corner of Sporgasse and Hauptplatz, next to the late Gothic arcades of the Luegg house (right and bottom right).

Unten: Der fünfgeschossige Bau des Großkaufhauses Kastner & Öhler wurde zwischen 1912 und 1914 vom Architektenduo Fellner und Helmer, die schon die Grazer Oper entworfen hatten, im Jugendstil errichtet.
Bottom: The five-storey building of the large department store "Kastner & Öhler" was erected in Art Nouveau style by the architects Fellner and Helmer, who had already designed the opera house.

Links: Der alte Innenhof eines Barockpalais in der Sackstraße 3–5 wurde zum Wintergarten des Hotels „Erzherzog Johann“ umgebaut.
Left: The old inner courtyard of the Baroque palace at Sackstraße 3–5 was turned into the winter garden of the “Erzherzog Johann” hotel.

Unten: Sackstraße Nummer 12: Hinter der Barockfassade verbirgt sich einer der schönsten Renaissance-Innenhöfe von Graz. Schon im 16. Jahrhundert war hier eine Trinkstube, deren Tradition das Restaurant „Krebsenkeller“ heute noch fortsetzt.
Bottom: Sackstraße 12: Behind the Baroque façade, there is one of the most beautiful Renaissance inner courtyards of Graz. As early as in the 16th century, it was home to a tap-room, whose tradition is still continued today by the “Krebsenkeller” restaurant.

Links: Fassade des Palais Attems – das einzige Barockpalais in Graz mit vollständig erhaltener Innenraumstruktur.
Left: Façade of Palais Attems – the only Baroque palace in Graz with a completely preserved interior structure.

Links: Die steile Prunkstiege im Palais Attems führt zu den Prunksälen in den oberen Geschossen, die heute für Veranstaltungen zur Verfügung stehen. Das Deckenfresko stammt von Franz Carl Remp (1706) und zeigt Merkur und Abundantia.
Left: The steep, magnificent staircase in Palais Attems leads to the splendid rooms in the upper storeys, which are used today for festive events. The ceiling fresco was painted by Franz Carl Remp (1706) and depicts Mercury and Abundantia.

Unten: Auf dem Schloßbergplatz befindet sich der Gastgarten der „Alten Münze“ und bietet schattige Ruhe vor dem steilen Anstieg auf den Schloßberg.
Bottom: At the beginning of Schlossbergplatz, there is the outside dining area of the “Alte Münze”, which provides for shady quiet before making the steep ascent up to the Schlossberg.

Die Stadtkrone – das kaiserliche Graz

Als der Habsburgerkaiser Ferdinand I. im Jahr 1564 starb, wurde sein Erbe unter seinen Söhnen aufgeteilt. Sein Jüngster, der 24-jährige Erzherzog Karl, erhielt Innerösterreich. Schon Jahre zuvor hatte er sich als Statthalter in Graz aufgehalten und die Erbhuldigung der Stände entgegengenommen. Mit seinem Regierungsantritt entwickelte sich Innerösterreich (Steiermark, Kärnten, Krain, Görz, Triest und Teile Istriens) zu einem selbstständigen Staatswesen, und Graz erlebte seine größte politische und kulturelle Blüte.

Als Residenzstadt von 1564 bis 1619 konzentrierte sich die gesamte weltliche und geistliche Macht des Landes in der Grazer Stadtkrone. Dort, wo einst Kaiser Friedrich III. auf einem Kirchhügel außerhalb der frühmittelalterlichen Marktsiedlung seine Stadtburg und den Dom errichtet hatte, erhielt die Stadt unter den Erzherzögen Karl und Ferdinand ihre architektonische Vollendung: Die Hof um Hof erweiterte Burg, der gotische Dom, das Mausoleum mit seiner manieristischen Fassade von Giovanni Pietro de Pomis und der venezianischen Kuppellandschaft sowie Universität und Kolleg der Jesuiten prägen heute noch das Grazer Stadtbild und ließen die ursprünglich getrennte bürgerliche Stadt und die imperiale Stadtkrone zusammenwachsen.

Links: Die venezianisch anmutende Kuppellandschaft des kaiserlichen Mausoleums stammt von Giovanni Pietro de Pomis, der 1614 mit dem Bau beauftragt wurde.
Left: The Venetian-style cupolas of the imperial mausoleum were created by Giovanni Pietro de Pomis, who was commissioned with their construction in 1614.

Eine landesfürstliche Zentralbehörde mit Hofkanzlei entstand. Viele Adelige und Wiener Beamte zogen in die neue Residenz und drängten das Bürgertum im Gesellschaftsleben zurück, was auch den Kampf zwischen katholischen und evangelischen Christen widerspiegelte. Denn die Ära Erzherzog Karls II. war vor allem geprägt durch die starke Ausbreitung des Protestantismus und den Abwehrkampf gegen die Türken. Und Karl benötigte die Hilfe des durchwegs protestantischen Adels gegen die Türkengefahr. So stimmte er der Religionspazifikation von 1572 zu, in der dem Adel und seinen Untertanen die Kultus- und Gewissensfreiheit bestätigt wurde. Die landesfürstlichen Städte und Märkte hingegen bekamen nur die Gewissensfreiheit zugestanden. Dennoch war die Lage für die katholische Kirche so bedrohlich, dass 1580 der Papst eine Nuntiatur in Graz einrichtete. 1572 hatte Karl schon die Jesuiten ins Land gerufen, die 1585 ihre Universität als Gegenpol zur 1570 errichteten evangelischen Stiftsschule (heute Paradeishof, wo auch Johannes Kepler von 1594 bis zu seiner Ausweisung im Jahr 1600 unterrichtete) gründeten. Die Rekatholisierung des ganzen Landes begann, der Machtkampf zwischen evangelischem Bürgertum und Adel auf der einen und dem Landesherrn, seinen Beamten und der katholischen Kirche auf der anderen Seite erlebte seinen Höhepunkt. Doch 1590 starb erst 50-jährig Karl II. Von seinen 15 Kindern war der zwölfjährige Ferdinand zur Nachfolge berufen und eben bei den Jesuiten in Ingolstadt zur Ausbildung. Nach einer kurzen Statthalterschaft, welche die Lage einigermaßen beruhigte, übernahm er 1596 die Herrschaft in Innerösterreich. Kompromisslos begann Ferdinand das Land wieder der katholischen Kirche zuzuführen. 1598 wurde die evangelische Stiftskirche geschlossen, 1599 die evangelischen Prediger des Landes verwiesen. Im Juli 1600 mussten die Grazer Bürger in der Pfarrkirche dem Luthertum abschwören – oder die Stadt verlassen. Als Kaiser Matthias 1619 kinderlos starb, wurde Erzherzog Ferdinand in Frankfurt zum Kaiser gewählt und zog als Ferdinand II. nach Wien. Der Glanz der Grazer Burg verblasste, ein Großteil der wertvollen Sammlungen wanderte in die Reichshauptstadt. Mitte des 19. Jahrhunderts wurde die Hälfte der Burgbauten, darunter auch die Prunktreppe Kaiser Ferdinands I., wegen Baufälligkeit abgerissen.

Die restlichen Teile der Burg sind seit 1922 Amtssitz des Landeshauptmanns von Steiermark.

The Crown of the City – Imperial Graz

When the Habsburg Emperor Ferdinand I died in 1564, his inheritance was shared out among his sons. His youngest son, the 24-year-old Archduke Karl, was given Inner Austria. He had already lived in Graz as a governor a few years back and had been acknowledged by the estates. From the time of his accession to power, Inner Austria (Styria, Carinthia, Carniola, Gorizia, Trieste, and parts of Istria) developed into an independent state, and Graz experienced its political and cultural heydays.
As the residential capital from 1564 to 1619, all of the secular and religious power of the empire was concentrated in the so-

called "crown of the town of Graz". On a church hill outside an early medieval market settlement, where Emperor Friedrich III had once built his town castle and the cathedral, the town now reached its architectural peak under the Archdukes Karl and Ferdinand. The castle, expanded by one courtyard after the other, the Gothic cathedral, the mausoleum with its Mannerist façade by Giovanni Pietro de Pomis, the landscape of Venetian cupolas, as well as the university and college of the Jesuits, still characterise Graz's cityscape today and have made the originally separated bourgeois town and the imperial "crown of the town" merge into one.
A sovereign, central authority including a court office emerged. Many noblemen and Viennese officials moved to the new residential capital and drove the bourgeoisie back into social life, which was also reflected in the struggle between Catholics and Protestants.
For the era of Archduke Karl II was above all characterised by the strong dissemination of Protestantism and the defensive struggle against the Turks. And Karl needed the help of the exclusively Protestant nobility against the danger posed by the Turks. Thus, in 1572 he acquiesced to the so-called religious pacification, granting the nobility and his subjects the freedom of religious education and practices and conscience. However, the towns and markets of the Archduke were only granted the freedom of conscience. However, the situation was still so threatening to the Catholic church that the pope appointed a nuncio in Graz in 1580. In 1572, Karl had already brought the Jesuits into his empire, who founded their university in 1585 as the antithesis to the Protestant collegiate school erected in 1570 (today's Paradeishof, where Johannes Kepler taught from 1594 until his expulsion in 1600). The Catholic Renewal of the whole empire began, and the power struggle between the Protestant bourgeoisie and the nobility, on the one hand, and the sovereign, his officials and the Catholic church, on the other hand, had reached its peak. But then, in 1590, Karl died at the early age of 50. Of his 15 children, 12-year-old Ferdinand, who at that time was being educated by the Jesuits in Ingolstadt, was appointed his successor. After a short governorship, which somewhat calmed down the situation, he took over the rule of Inner Austria in 1596. Uncompromisingly, Ferdinand began to lead his empire back to the Catholic church. The Protestant collegiate church was closed down in 1598, and Protestant preachers were exiled in 1599. In July of 1600, the citizens of Graz had to renounce Lutheranism in the parish church – or leave the city immediately. When Emperor Matthias died in 1619 without leaving an heir, Archduke Ferdinand was crowned Emperor in Frankfurt and moved to Vienna as Ferdinand II. The splendour of Graz's castle faded, and a major part of the precious collections was transferred to the imperial capital. In the middle of the 19th century, half of the castle complex, including the magnificent staircase of Ferdinand I, had to be pulled down due to its poor condition.
The remaining parts of the castle have been used as the official residence of the provincial governor of Styria since 1922.

Rechts: Das spätgotische Netzrippengewölbe des Doms trägt neben der Jahreszahl 1450 auch Kaiser Friedrichs III. rätselhafte Devise „AEIOU".
Right: The late Gothic rib vault of the cathedral bears the date 1450 as well as the mysterious motto "AEIOU" of Emperor Friedrich III.

Links oben: Blick in den Gruftraum des Mausoleums von Kaiser Ferdinand II., hier dominiert der Marmorsarkophag mit den Figuren seiner Eltern.
Above left: View into the crypt of the mausoleum of Emperor Ferdinand II. Here, the marble sarcophagus with figures of his parents dominates the room.

Links: Manieristisch verschachtelte Giebel sind das besondere Kennzeichen des Mausoleums, das als eines der bedeutendsten Bauwerke des frühen 17. Jahrhunderts in Österreich gilt.
Left: The nested gables in Mannerist style are the distinctive characteristics of the mausoleum, which is considered to be one of Austria's most important constructions of the early 17th century.

Oben: Blick vom Stadtpark auf die Kuppellandschaft des Mausoleums samt Campanile, die im Einklang mit dem Dom (rechts) und der Burg als Grazer Stadtkrone bezeichnet wird.
Above: View from the City Park of the mausoleum's cupolas including the campanile, which, together with the cathedral (right) and the castle, are called the "Crown of the City of Graz".

Rechts: Die Gruftkapelle mit dem Marmorsarg und den Liegefiguren Erzherzog Karls und seiner Gattin Maria Anna von Bayern, den Eltern Ferdinands. Sie gilt als erster überkuppelter Ovalbau außerhalb Italiens.
Right: The crypt chapel with the marble sarcophagus and the reclining figures of Archduke Karl and his wife Maria Anna von Bayern, Ferdinand's parents. It is regarded as the first oval construction with a cupola outside of Italy.

Oben: Der heilige Christophorus, Fresko um 1460/70, im nördlichen Seitenschiff des Domes.
Above: St. Christopher, fresco around 1460/70, in the northern aisle of the cathedral.

Rechts: Unter Friedrich III. erfolgte zwischen 1438 und 1462 der Bau der spätgotischen Pfarrkirche St. Ägydius, 1577 wurde sie an die Jesuiten übergeben, die sie mit prächtiger barocker Innenausstattung umgestalteten. Seit 1786 ist sie Domkirche der Diözese Graz-Seckau. Das spätgotische Kirchengebäude steht mit seiner schlichten Form ganz in der Bautradition der Bettelorden, einzig das Westportal ist reich gegliedert (rechts oben).
Right: The construction of the late Gothic parish church of St. Ägydius took place under Friedrich III between 1438 and 1462. In 1577, it was handed over to the Jesuits, who redesigned its interior in splendid Baroque style. Since 1786, it has been the cathedral church of the Diocese of Graz-Seckau. With its simple shape, the late Gothic church building is consistent with the building tradition of the mendicant orders. Only the west portal is lavishly structured (above right).

Oben: Blick in den gotischen Domchor mit reicher barocker Ausstattung, die vom Hochaltar noch dominiert wird – eine der bedeutendsten barocken Altaranlagen der Steiermark.
Above: View of the cathedral's Gothic choir with its rich Baroque furnishings, which is still dominated by the high altar – one of Styria's most important Baroque altars.

Bis auf das reich verzierte Westportal (links) war die Kirche außen eher schmucklos. Um sie zu verschönern, wurden die schlichten Mauern mit Fresken versehen. Als einziges Bild ist heute noch an der Südseite das berühmte gotische Landplagenbild des Thomas von Villach zu sehen, das von Umwelteinflüssen schrecklich mitgenommen war und nun aufwändig restauriert wurde. Diese älteste Grazer Stadtansicht erinnert an die Gottesplagen, die die Stadt heimsuchten: Heuschrecken, Türken und Pest (1485).
Except for the richly decorated west portal (left), the church was rather plain on the outside. In order to beautify it, the plain walls were provided with frescoes. The famous Gothic plague fresco by Thomas von Villach is the only fresco left on the southern side. Once badly damaged by environmental influences, it has now been lavishly restored. The oldest view of the city of Graz reminds one of God's plagues that afflicted the city: locusts, the Turks, and the plague (1485).

Links: Der romantische Innenhof im Haus des Deutschen Ritterordens in der nahen Sporgasse zählt mit seinen spätgotischen Säulen und Arkadengängen zu den schönsten Höfen der Stadt.

Left: In nearby Sporgasse, the romantic inner courtyard of the House of the Order of the Teutonic Knights, with its late Gothic columns and arcades, is among the city's most beautiful courtyards.

Links: Das mächtige fünfgeschossige Jesuitenkollegium umfasst mit seiner Strenge und Schlichtheit den mit 1300 Quadratmetern größten Innenhof der Altstadt. Hier wurde 1585 von Erzherzog Karl II., dem Vater Ferdinands, die Grazer Universität gegründet.
Left: The mighty five-storey Jesuit Collegium surrounds the largest inner courtyard (1,300 m²) in the historic centre of Graz with its strictness and plainness. This is the place where Archduke Karl II, Ferdinand's father, founded Graz University in 1585.

Rechts: Das wohl bedeutendste und auch berühmteste Baudenkmal des Spätmittelalters findet man in der Grazer Burg, wenn man den Burghof durchquert, links im Turm vor der Durchfahrt in den zweiten Hof: die gotische Doppelwendeltreppe aus Stein, die 1499 im Auftrag Kaiser Maximilians I., des Sohnes von Friedrich III., errichtet wurde.
Right: The most important and most famous architectural monument of the late Middle Ages can be found in the castle of Graz by crossing the castle courtyard and turning left into the tower before the passage to the second courtyard: The Gothic double spiral staircase made of stone, which was commissioned by Emperor Maximilian I, the son of Friedrich III, and built in 1499.

Oben: Der Lambrechter Hof am umgestalteten Freiheitsplatz mit dem Denkmal von Kaiser Franz I. Der nun verkehrsberuhigte Platz ist mit seiner geschlossenen Bebauung aus Spätklassizismus und Biedermeier nicht nur einer der schönsten Plätze von Graz, sondern auch ein Eldorado der Kaffeehausgeher, rechts das Szenelokal „Fink". Daneben in der anschließenden Hofgasse die älteste Bäckerei (1569) der Stadt mit dem berühmten Portal aus Eichenholz mit Nussholzeinlagen von 1894.

Above: The Lambrechter Hof on the redesigned Freiheitsplatz featuring the monument of Emperor Franz I. Now a slow-traffic zone, the square, with its cohesive building structure in late Classicist and Biedermeier style, is not only one of Graz' most beautiful squares, but also an El Dorado for coffeehouse guests. On the right, there is the popular "Fink" café-bar. Next to it, in the adjacent Hofgasse, there is Graz' oldest bakery (1569), with its famous portal made of oak-wood with walnut inlays dating from 1894.

Links: Das Steiermärkische Landesarchiv auf dem Karmeliterplatz im „Haus der Geschichte“, die „Sonnenuhr“ stammt von Wolfgang Buchner (2000).
Left: The Styrian Provincial Archive on Karmeliterplatz in the “House of History”. The sundial was created by Wolfgang Buchner (2000).

Unten: Der „Türke“ im barocken Palais Saurau in der Sporgasse Nr. 25. Beachtenswert ist auch der Innenhof dieses Palais mit seiner Murnockerlpflasterung und den alten Renaissance-Elementen sowie das Portal mit dem barocken schmiedeeisernen Oberlichtgitter.
Bottom: The “Turk” in the Baroque Palais Saurau at Sporgasse No. 25. Also worthy of note are the inner courtyard of the palace with its paving of small, round stones from the river Mur (the so-called “Murnockerl”) and its old Renaissance elements, as well as the portal with its Baroque, wrought-iron fanlight grille.

Rechts: Das zwischen 1582 und 1614 erbaute Paulustor am Beginn des Stadtparks gilt heute als die bedeutendste Renaissance-Toranlage im ganzen deutschen Sprachraum. Zu beiden Seiten des alten Stadttores die steinernen Wappen von Erzherzog Ferdinand und seiner Gattin Maria Anna von Bayern.
Right: The Paulustor gate at the entrance to the City Park was built between 1582 and 1614 and today is considered to be the most important Renaissance gate construction in the whole German-speaking area. On both sides of the old city gate, there are the stone coats of arms of Archduke Ferdinand and his wife Maria Anna von Bayern.

Links: Zentrum des Stadtparks ist seit 1873 der Stadtparkbrunnen, den der Grazer Stadtverschönerungsverein auf der Weltausstellung in Wien erwarb: Ein von Jean-Baptiste Jules Klagmann entworfener gusseiserner Brunnen, der mit reichlichem Figurenschmuck versehen ist.
Left: Since 1873, the centre of the City Park has been its fountain, which was purchased by the Graz City Beautification Society at the World Exhibition in Vienna: a cast iron fountain designed by Jean-Baptiste Jules Klagmann and richly decorated with figures.

Oben: Sandsteinfigur am Rand des Parks neben dem alten Rest des romantischen Burggrabens.
Above: Sandstone figure at the edge of the park next to the old remains of the romantic moat.

Im Reichsgesetzblatt vom 20. November 1868 wurde das Gesetz veröffentlicht, das die Grundlage bildete für den Tausch der vom Militär als Übungsgelände genutzten Glacisgründe mit dem Feliferhof im Westen von Graz. 1872 war es dann soweit: Die Stadt unter ihrem Bürgermeister Moritz Ritter von Franck erwarb gegen den Willen vieler Bürger, die sich um Moral und Sicherheit sorgten, die Gründe, um sie als Stadtpark – die grüne Lunge der Stadt – anzulegen.

In the Imperial Law Gazette of November 20, 1868, a law was published that provided the basis for the trade of the Glacis grounds, used by the military back then as their training grounds, for the Feliferhof in the west of Graz. In 1872, its time had come: Against the wishes of many citizens, who were concerned about morality and safety, the city under its mayor Moritz Ritter von Franck purchased the grounds and turned them into the City Park – the green lungs of the city.

Links: Karl-Franzens-Universität: Nach Aufhebung des Jesuitenordens und damit auch der alten Grazer Universität neben dem Dom im Jahr 1782 wurde erst wieder 1827 von Kaiser Franz I. die Grazer Universität neu errichtet. 1891/95 wurde das heutige Hauptgebäude im Geidorfviertel erbaut.

Left: Karl-Franzens University: After the abolition of the Jesuit order and thus the closing-down of the old university situated next to the cathedral in 1782, the University of Graz was re-established by Emperor Franz I in 1827. Today's main building was built in the Geidorf quarter in 1891/95.

Oben links: Die Gewächshäuser des Botanischen Gartens der Karl-Franzens-Universität in der Schubertstraße: Eine elegante Komposition aus Glas und Aluminium, die 1995 nach den Plänen des Architekten Volker Giencke vor der Kulisse des alten Villenviertels errichtet wurde.
Above left: The greenhouses of the Botanical Garden of the Karl-Franzens University in Schubertstraße: An elegant composition of glass and aluminium, which was erected in front of the backdrop of the old exclusive residential district in 1995 according to the plans of architect Volker Giencke.

Oben Mitte: Das von Günter Domenig und Hermann Eisenköck geplante Resowi-Zentrum für die mehr als 14.000 Studierenden der Rechts-, Sozial- und Wirtschaftswissenschaftlichen Fakultät ist ein hervorragendes Beispiel der modernen Grazer Architektur.
Above centre: Planned by Günter Domenig and Hermann Eisenköck, the so-called "Resowi-Zentrum", for the more than 14,000 students of the Faculty of Legal, Social and Economic Studies, is an excellent example of modern architecture in Graz.

Oben rechts: Die „Biokatalyse", ein Labor- und Bürogebäude der TU-Graz, Planung: Ernst Giselbrecht.
The so-called "Biocatalysis", a laboratory and office building of the TU Graz, planning: Ernst Giselbrecht.

Der Schloßberg

Mitten aus dem Grazer Becken erhebt sich mit 473 Metern Seehöhe der Dolomitfelsen des Schloßbergs über Graz. Wuchtige 123 Meter überragt er den Hauptplatz und bietet Schutz.
Im frühen Mittelalter bauten hier slawische Bewohner eine kleine Burg (slawisch gradec), die Graz ihren Namen gab.
Durch diese Festung wurden die Furt über die Mur und der Handelsweg gesichert, der hier von der am Westrand des Grazer Beckens in Nord-Süd-Richtung verlaufenden Römerstraße nach Osten abzweigte. Eine im Mittelalter auf dem Schloßbergplateau errichtete Burg wurde ab 1544 unter Domenico dell'Aglio nach dem italienischen Bastionensystem zu einer mächtigen Festung gegen die Türken ausgebaut, die von keinem Feind eingenommen werden konnte.
Auch 1809 konnte Major Franz von Hackher den Schloßberg gegen Napoleons Revolutionsarmee erfolgreich verteidigen. „Das Feuer der Franzosen dauerte sieben Tage und Nächte fast ununterbrochen fort. Man zählte neunzig Kanonenschüsse in einer Stunde", berichtet der k. k. Feldmarschallleutnant Wilhelm von Gebler in seiner „Geschichte des Herzogthums Steiermark" aus dem Jahr 1862. Nach drei Wochen erfolgloser Bestürmung zogen die Franzosen am 21. Juni Richtung Norden ab. Aber bereits zwei Tage später kam es neuerlich zu heftigen Kämpfen um Graz, die bis zum Znaimer Waffenstillstand am 12. Juli andauerten. Im Friedensvertrag von Schönbrunn verlangte Napoleon die Schleifung der uneinnehmbaren Festung. Nur der 1559/69 aus einem mittelalterlichen Wehrturm umgebaute Feuerwachturm (Uhrturm, das Wahrzeichen von Graz) und der achteckige Renaissanceturm, der 1588 als Glockenturm („Liesl") zur romanischen Thomaskapelle erbaut wurde, konnten von den Grazern durch eine Lösegeldzahlung von 2840 Gulden gerettet werden. Bis auf drei Basteien wurden alle anderen Befestigungsanlagen umgehend von den Franzosen gesprengt. „Nur die St. Thomaskapelle ließen die Franzosen als vermeintliches Römerdenkmal stehen. Sie fiel erst später einheimischem Vandalismus zum Opfer", weiß Gebler. Heute findet man ihre Fundamente direkt hinter dem Glockenturm wieder freigelegt.
Auf den Trümmern der alten Festungsanlage ließen die steirischen Stände bereits 1818 erste Wege mit Baumbepflanzungen errichten. Viele Pläne wurden für die Nutzung des Schloßbergs geschmiedet, bevor die Landstände 1839 die Umgestaltung in einen englischen Garten mit ganzflächiger Begrünung genehmigten. Bereits 1841 war mit Unterstützung des Militärs der Umbau zu einem großen Park mit Pavillons und Schweizerhaus fertig.
Heute bietet der Schloßberg mehr als 1700 Tier- und Pflanzenarten Lebensraum. Und die Besucher haben von hier aus den wohl schönsten Blick auf die berühmte Dachlandschaft der Grazer Altstadt.
Aber auch das Innere des Berges ist voller Leben: Ab 1943 wurde ein weitläufiges Stollensystem von sechs Kilometer Länge errichtet, das im Zweiten Weltkrieg als Luftschutzstollen diente. Im Jahr 2000 wurden zwei dieser Stollen zum „Dom im Berg" ausgebaut, der nun als felsige Kulisse für zahlreiche Großveranstaltungen Verwendung findet.
Als Aufstiegshilfen stehen die 1894 errichtete Schloßbergbahn (Talstation Kaiser-Franz-Josef-Kai 38) und der von 1914 bis 1918 mit Hilfe russischer Kriegsgefangener errichtete „Kriegssteig", ausgehend vom Schloßbergplatz (wo auch das in seinen Fundamenten älteste Gebäude von Graz, der Reinerhof, steht), zur Verfügung. Und seit 2000 führt von hier auch ein architektonisch bemerkenswerter Lift im Berg direkt zum Uhrturm. Auch der Hauptstollen quer durch den ganzen Berg vom Schloßbergplatz bis zum Karmeliterplatz wurde begehbar gemacht und bildet jetzt eine Kulturachse quer durch die Stadt.

Links: Der Schloßbergsteig oder Kriegssteig, der während des Ersten Weltkrieges von Soldaten und russischen Kriegsgefangenen gebaut wurde, führt über 260 Stufen vom Schloßbergplatz steil zum Uhrturm.
Left: The "Schlossbergsteig" or "Kriegssteig", which was erected by soldiers and Russian prisoners of war during World War I, is a steep path with 260 steps leading up from Schlossbergpatz to the Clock Tower.

The Schlossberg

In the midst of the Graz Basin, the dolomite rock of the Schlossberg rises above Graz, 473 metres above sea level. With its mighty 123 metres, it towers above the Hauptplatz and provides protection.
In the early Middle Ages, Slavic inhabitants built a small castle here (gradec in Slavic), which gave Graz its name. This fortress protected the ford across the Mur and the trade route via the Roman road running north to south along the western edge of the Graz Basin that branched off to the East here. Starting in 1544, Domenico dell'Aglio expanded and fortified a castle, which in the Middle Ages was erected on

the Schlossberg plateau, into a mighty fortress against the Turks according to the Italian bastion system. No enemy ever succeeded in taking this fortress.
Also in 1809, Major Franz von Hackher could successfully defend the Schlossberg against Napoleon's revolutionary army. "The French bombardment went on almost incessantly for seven days and nights. Ninety cannon shots were counted in one hour", reported Wilhelm von Gebler, Lieutenant Field Marshal, in his Geschichte des Herzogthums Steiermark (History of the Duchy of Styria) written in 1862. After three unsuccessful weeks of assault, the French troops withdrew and moved north on June 21. However, two days later, there was heavy fighting again over Graz, which continued until the Armistice of Znaim on July 12. In the Peace Treaty of Schönbrunn, Napoleon demanded that the impregnable fortress be razed to the ground. Only the fire watch-tower (the clock tower, Graz's landmark), which was the result of the reconstruction of a fortified tower in 1559/69, as well as the octagonal Renaissance tower, which was added to the Romanesque Thomas chapel as a bell tower (Liesl) in 1588, could be saved by the inhabitants of Graz by paying a ransom of 2840 guilders. Except for three bastions, all the other fortifications were immediately blown up by the French. "The French only left the St. Thomas chapel as a supposedly Roman monument. Only later did it fall victim to local vandalism", said Gebler. Today, one can find its exposed foundations directly behind the bell tower.
On the ruins of the old fortifications, the Styrian estates had the first paths lined with trees laid out as early as in 1818. Many a plan had been hatched for the use of the Schlossberg, until the estates approved of its conversion into an English landscape garden with greenery covering the whole area in 1839. As early as in 1841, it was converted into a large park including pavilions and a Swiss style house with the help of the army.
Today the Schlossberg is home to more than 1700 animal and plant species. And from up there, visitors certainly have the most beautiful view of the famous roof-scape of the historic part of Graz.
But the interior of the mountain is also full of life: Starting in 1943, an extensive, six kilometre long tunnel was constructed, which served as air raid tunnels during World War II. In 2000, two of these tunnels were converted into the Dom im Berg (Dome in the Mountain), which now provides the rocky backdrop for numerous large events.
For easy access, there is the Schlossberg funicular (valley station at Kaiser-Franz-Josef-Kai 38), constructed in 1894, and the path called the Felsensteig, which was erected with the help of Russian prisoners of war between 1914 and 1918. It leads up from the Schlossbergplatz (where the Reinerhof building, with Graz's oldest foundations, is also situated). From here, a lift in the mountain, boasting remarkable architecture, has taken visitors directly up to the clock tower since 2000. The main tunnel, which cuts through the whole mountain, from Schlossbergplatz to Karmeliterplatz, was also made accessible and now forms a cultural axis running right through the city.

Rechts: Der gläserne Lift im Schloßbergstollen, der spektakulär innerhalb des Berges vom Schloßbergplatz zum Uhrturm führt.
Right: The glass lift in the Schlossberg gallery inside the "mountain" is a spectacular way of travelling from Schlossbergplatz up to the Clock Tower.

LIFT
LIFT

Rechts: Der Schloßberg erhebt sich mit 473 Metern Seehöhe stolze 123 Meter über den Hauptplatz und gilt als der grüne Hausberg der Grazer, von dem aus man die beste Aussicht auf die Altstadt genießt. Hier der Blick von Osten auf die unbebaute Rückseite des Berges, links im Bild der Glockenturm „Liesl".
Right: The Schlossberg, considered to be the green hometown hill of Graz, proudly rises up to 473 metres above sea level and 123 metres above Hauptplatz, and offers the best view of the old part of the city. Here, a view from the east of the undeveloped back side of the "mountain", and, on the left, a view of the bell tower called "Liesl".

Unten: Ein ganz besonderes Erlebnis mit Weitblick ist die Einkehr ins Terrassenrestaurant auf dem Schloßberg gegenüber dem Glockenturm.
Below: Making a stop at the terrace restaurant on top of the Schlossberg opposite the bell tower is a very special experience that provides guests with an excellent view.

Rechts: Der 1588 erbaute Glockenturm wird von den Grazern liebevoll wie seine Glocke „Liesl“ genannt, im Kellergewölbe befand sich das Gefängnis der Festung.
Right: Built in 1588, the bell tower, as well as its bell, are lovingly referred to as “Liesl” by the inhabitants of Graz. In the underground vault, there was the fortress’ prison.

Rechts unten: Die „Liesl“ oder „Siebenglocke“, der Sage nach 1587 aus 101 türkischen Kanonenkugeln gegossen, hängt im obersten Stockwerk und ist mit ihren 4632 Kilogramm die drittschwerste Glocke der Steiermark.
Bottom right: According to legend, the “Liesl” or “Siebenglocke” was cast out of 101 Turkish cannonballs in 1587. It hangs on the top storey and weighing 4,632 kilograms, it is Styria’s third-heaviest bell.

Ganz oben: Das Uhrwerk des Uhrturms von 1712, rechts das Zifferblatt, das beweist, dass die Uhren in Graz anders zu gehen scheinen und doch stimmen – hier sind die Zeiger vertauscht, weil ursprünglich nur ein (großer) Zeiger die Stunden anzeigte.
Above top: The clock mechanism of the Clock Tower dating from 1712, and, on the right, there is the dial which gives proof of the fact that the clocks in Graz seem to move otherwise and yet are still accurate – here, the hands are switched, since there was originally only one (huge) hand showing the hours.

Mitte: Die neuen Wagen der Schloßbergbahn, die mit 60 Prozent Steigung zum Terrassenrestaurant führt.
Centre: The new cars of the Schlossberg funicular. At a 60 degree angle, the funicular runs up to the terrace restaurant.

Unten: Der gläserne Lift im Bergstollen. Daneben das Cafe „Aiola" mit seinem herrlichen Terrassengarten neben dem Uhrturm.
Bottom: The glass lift in the "mountain" gallery. Beside it, next to the Clock Tower, Café "Aiola", with its magnificent terrace garden.

Rechts: Der Uhrturm ist das 28 Meter hohe Wahrzeichen der Stadt und das wohl beliebteste Fotomotiv aller Touristen. Er wurde 1559/69 unter Einbeziehung eines mittelalterlichen Wehrturms als Wachturm für die Feuermeldung errichtet und beinhaltet drei Glocken, darunter die älteste von Graz aus dem Jahr 1382. Um den Turm führt ein hölzerner Gang mit drei Erkern.

Right: The 28 metre tall Clock Tower is the city's landmark and certainly the most popular photo motif of tourists. It was erected in 1559/69 by adding to a medieval fortified tower used as a fire watch-tower and it holds three bells, among them the city's oldest dating back to 1382. There is a wooden corridor with three bay windows running around the tower.

Links oben: Im Jahr 2000 wurden zwei Stollen des weit verzweigten Luftschutzstollensystems aus dem Zweiten Weltkrieg zum „Dom im Berg“ ausgebaut. 20 Meter breit, 12 Meter hoch und 28 Meter lang ist der über 500 Quadratmeter große Raum im Felsmassiv, der zum exklusiven Veranstaltungsort wurde.

Above left: In 2000, two tunnels of the widely branching network of air raid tunnels from World War II were built up into the "Dom im Berg". This exclusive event venue is a hall in the rock massif with more than 500 m² and is 20 metres wide, 12 metres tall and 28 metres long.

Links unten: Tief durch das Innere des Berges führt der Zugang zum „Dom im Berg“, der gleichzeitig auch ein Durchgang vom Schloßbergplatz zum anderen Ende des Berges kurz vor dem Karmeliterplatz ist.

Bottom left: The passageway leading to the "Dom im Berg" runs deep into the interior of the "mountain" and is at the same time the connection from Schlossbergplatz to the other side of the mountain, right in front of Karmeliterplatz.

Rechts: Einer der beliebtesten Plätze zum Genießen – das idyllische Lokal im Starckehäuschen, 1572 als Pulverturm erbaut, 1818 zum Winzerhäuschen umfunktioniert.
Right: One of the most popular places for culinary treats – the idyllic restaurant in the little Starcke house, which was built in 1572 as a powder tower and was turned into a wine growing house in 1818.

Oben: Die Stall- oder Kanonenbastei, 1544 von Domenico dell'Aglio als erster Festungsabschnitt erbaut, ist 20 Meter hoch und hat sechs Meter dicke Mauern. Von hier eröffnet sich ein herrlicher Blick auf das Grazer Feld. Darunter die Kasematten der Stallbastei, die im Rahmen einer Schloßbergführung zugänglich sind.
Above: The stable or cannon bastion, which was built by Domenico dell'Aglio as the first section of the fortress in 1544, is 20 metres high and has walls that are six metres thick. Here, a magnificent view of the Graz plain opens up. Beneath the bastion, there are the casemates, which are only accessible as part of a guided tour of the Schlossberg.

Blicke über die Stadt: Vom Palais Attems über das Kunsthaus Richtung Südwesten (rechts), über das Rathaus gegen Süden (rechts oben), nochmals der Schwenk nach Westen mit dem 2003-Haus auf dem Mariahilferplatz im Vordergrund sowie über Dom und Mausoleum gegen Osten zur Herz-Jesu-Kirche.
A view of the city: From Palais Attems to the Kunsthaus (House of Art) towards the south-east (right), of the city hall towards the south (above right), again, panning to the west, a view of the 2003 house in the foreground on Mariahilferplatz, as well as of the cathedral and the mausoleum towards Herz-Jesu church to the east.

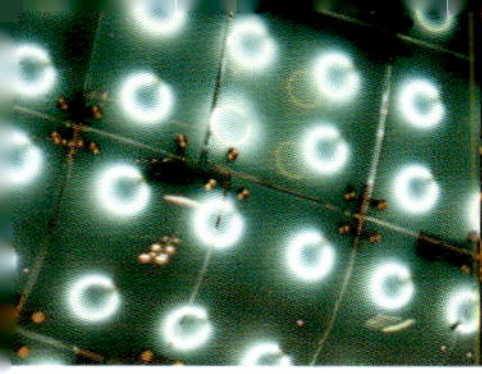

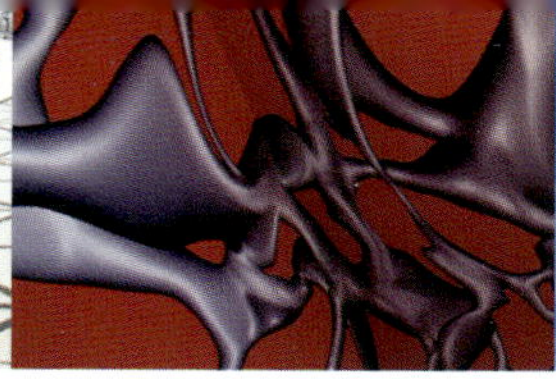

Die Kulturhauptstadt

Es hatte alles schon sehr viel versprechend begonnen, als am 11. Jänner 2003 mehr als 80.000 begeisterte Menschen bei Eis, Schnee und klirrender Kälte in der altehrwürdigen Grazer Innenstadt der offiziellen Eröffnung des Europäischen Kulturhauptstadtjahres beiwohnten. Über dem Schloßberg erleuchtete ein viel bestauntes japanisches Feuerwerk den Abendhimmel. Und Graz hatte sich auch entsprechend herausgeputzt, ja geradezu neu eingekleidet.
Dem Uhrturm wurde auf Zeit ein Schatten zur Seite gestellt, der heute im Shopping Center Seiersberg südlich von Graz steht. Neben der barocken Mariensäule am Eisernen Tor zu Beginn der belebten Herrengasse stand einige Jahre ein schlanker Lift, der den neugierigen Besucher in Augenhöhe mit der vergoldeten Marienstatue führte, die einst von den Grazer Bürgern aus Dankbarkeit für die Errettung vor den Türken errichtet worden war. Die „Kunst-Insel" des New Yorker Künstlers Vito Acconci schwimmt spektakulär, aber gut verankert, in der Mur und ist durch zwei schlanke Stege mit beiden Flussufern verbunden. Die in den 60er Jahren durch neue Uferstraßen vom städtischen Leben völlig abgeschnittenen Murufer wurden neu erschlossen, romantische Murpromenaden lassen nun den Fluss aus nächster Nähe erleben und verlocken zu gemütlichen Spaziergängen. Und als sensationellster Bau entstand nach jahrelanger Standortsuche am rechten Murufer in Sichtweite der Murinsel und im direkten Anschluss an das denkmalgeschützte und neu renovierte „Eiserne Haus" (eine nun völlig ausgehöhlte Gusseisenkonstruktion von 1848) ein Kunsthaus, das von außen auch international keine Vergleiche zu scheuen braucht.
Wie eine riesige Blase schwebt nach den Plänen der Londoner Architekten Peter Cook und Colin Fournier der mit bläulich schimmernden Acrylplatten verkleidete, auch als „friendly alien" bezeichnete Bau über dem Murufer des Lendkais.
Nach dem Entwurf von Klaus Kada entstand auf dem Gelände der Grazer Messe unter einem – in mehrfachem Sinne – hervorragenden Dach eine multifunktionale Stadthalle für alle.
Dazu gibt es mit der Helmut-List-Halle in der Waagner-Biró-Straße einen akustisch nahezu perfekten Aufführungsort moderner (steirischer herbst) und klassischer (Styriarte) Musik. Ein Literaturhaus als Zubau des Kulturhauses wurde in der Elisabethstraße errichtet, im Augarten entstand das Kindermuseum.
Graz war 2003 ein kultureller Knotenpunkt von Avantgarde und Tradition – vor der einzigartigen Altstadtkulisse mit ihren reizvollen Gastgärten und gemütlichen Straßencafés, in die sich die Menschenmassen vor der brütenden Hitze dieses Jahrhundertsommers flüchteten. Überall sah man ein bisschen Kunst. Schon an den Autobahneinfahrten winkten ein Jahr lang künstliche Arme den Autofahrern entgegen und mutierte in Fotomontagen der ehemalige Sturm-Graz-Trainerphilosoph Ivica Osim in den genialen Musiksohn der Stadt, Nikolaus Harnoncourt. Und die große neue Bahnhofshalle ist auch nach dem Kulturhauptstadtjahr noch immer ein einziger riesiger Bilderrahmen für Peter Koglers monumental-dekorative Illusionsräume in den Farben Schwarz, Rot und Weiß.
Natürlich haben es Projekte von so gewaltiger Dimension wie Kunsthaus und Murinsel nicht leicht: Sie kosten sehr, sehr viel Geld, stürzen ganze Städte jahrelang in tiefe Schulden und sind in ihrer modern-avantgardistischen Gestaltung auch noch sehr umstritten. Aber es war immer schon das scheinbar Unnötige, das den Glanz und die Attraktivität einer Stadt ausmachte, nie das Normale und Alltäglich-Biedere. Denn seien wir ehrlich: Wer hat schon den seinerzeit ebenfalls heftig angefeindeten Pariser Eiffelturm oder das Brüsseler Atomium wirklich gebraucht?

Links: Das Spiel der architektonischen Gegensätze zeigt sich besonders reizvoll am harmonischen Nebeneinander der „Nozzels" an der Oberseite des Kunsthauses mit den Gebäuden der alten Murvorstadt.
Left: The play of architectural opposites is most attractively revealed in the harmonious juxtaposition of the "nozzles" on top of the Kunsthaus and the buildings of the old Mur suburbs.

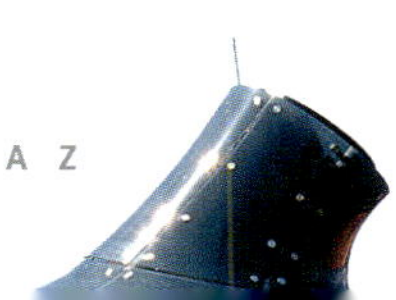

The Cultural Capital

Everything started out very promisingly, when on January 11, 2003, more than 80,000 enthusiastic people braved the ice, snow and biting cold to attend the official opening of the European Cultural Capital Year in the venerable old part of the City of Graz. Marvellous Japanese fireworks lit up the night sky above the Schlossberg. And Graz itself had accordingly been decked out; indeed it presented itself in a totally new design.
The clock tower was temporarily given a shadow, which today is to be seen in the Seiersberg shopping centre south of Graz. Right beside the Baroque column of Mary on the Eisernes Tor at the entrance to the

bustling Herrengasse, there was a slim lift taking curious visitors up to eye-level with the gilded statue of Mary. The inhabitants of Graz once erected it out of gratitude for their salvation from the Turks. The "island of art" by the New York artist Vito Acconci floats spectacularly, but well anchored, in the river Mur and is connected to both banks via two narrow foot-bridges. The banks of the Mur, which in the 60s were completely cut off from city life by new riverside streets, have been made accessible anew. Now romantic Mur promenades let people experience the river up close and invite them to go for a stroll. After years of searching for the right location, the most sensational building was erected on the right bank of the Mur in sight of the Murinsel (Island in the Mur) and directly connected to the newly renovated Eisernes Haus (Iron House; now a completely hollowed out cast iron construction from 1848 and put under an order for the preservation of historic buildings and monuments): the Kunsthaus (House of Art), which does not have to be afraid of any international comparison. Like a huge bubble, the building, also called the "friendly alien", hovers over the bank of the Mur of the Lendkai. According to the plans of the London-based architects Peter Cook and Colin Fournier, it was covered with a shimmering skin of blue acrylic panels. According to the design of Klaus Kada, a multi-functional event hall, the Stadthalle, was erected on the grounds of the Graz Trade Fair under an outstanding roof, in more than one sense of the word.
In addition, the Helmut-List-Halle on Waagner-Biró-Strasse provides a nearly perfect acoustic performance location for modern (steirischer herbst) and classical (Styriarte) music. A Literaturhaus (House of Literature) was added to the Kulturhaus (House of Culture) on Elisabethstrasse; and the children's museum was built in the Augarten Park.
In 2003, Graz was a cultural intersection of the avant-garde and tradition – in front of the unique backdrop of the historic part of the city with its charming and cosy pavement and street cafés, in which the crowds took refuge from the boiling heat of the summer of the century. There was a little bit of art to be seen everywhere. Already at the slip roads into the city, drivers were waved at by artificial arms for a year, and photo montages made the former Sturm Graz football trainer and philosopher, Ivica Osim, morph into the city's inspired musical son, Nikolaus Harnoncourt. And after the Cultural Capital Year, the great new train station hall is still one giant frame for Peter Kogler's monumental-decorative illusionary spaces in black, red and white. Of course, projects of such huge dimensions as the Kunsthaus and the Murinsel do not have it easy. They cost a lot of money, plunge whole cities into deep debt for years, and, in addition, they are very controversial due to their modern and avant-garde design. However, it has always been the seemingly unnecessary, that make up the splendour and attractiveness of a city, never the normal and unsophisticated.
Let us be honest: Who has ever really needed the Eiffel Tower in Paris or the Atomium in Brussels, which also met with severe hostility at the time?

Rechts: Alt und Neu in gespiegelter Brechung am Beispiel des wehrhaften Turmes der Franziskanerkirche (1643) im Glas des Kunsthauses (2003) auf dem anderen Murufer.
Right: Old and new in a reflected refraction: the fortified tower of the Franciscan church (1643), mirrored in the glass of the Kunsthaus (2003) on the opposite bank of the Mur.

Oben: Das Kunsthaus, die riesige blau schimmernde Blase der Londoner Architekten Peter Cook und Colin Fournier, in eindrucksvoller abendlicher Harmonie mit dem historischen Ambiente der alten Murvorstadt.
Above: The Kunsthaus (House of Art), the huge blue shimmering bubble of the London-based architects Peter Cook and Colin Fournier, in impressive evening harmony with the historical ambience of the old Mur suburbs.

Links: Vom Foyer aus führt die „Pin“ bzw. der „Travelator“, ein aufsteigendes Fahrband, zu den Ausstellungsräumen in den Obergeschossen und zur „Needle“.
Left: An ascending moving walkway, the so-called “Pin” or “Travelator”, takes visitors from the foyer up to the exhibition halls in the upper storeys and to the “Needle”.

Rechts: Der „Friendly Alien", der 2003 spektakulär am Murufer landete, als touristisches Fotomotiv von allen Seiten. Rechts oben in über 16 Meter Höhe und rundum verglast die „Needle", unten der Blick vom Terrassencafé des Kaufhauses Kastner & Öhler auf dem anderen Murufer.
Right: The "Friendly Alien", which spectacularly landed on the bank of the Mur in 2003, as a tourist photo motif from all sides: above right, the "Needle", more than 16 metres above ground and glassed in, and below, a view from the terrace café of the Kastner & Öhler department store of the opposite bank of the river.

Jetzt hat auch Graz seine Murinsel – der Kulturhauptstadt 2003 sei Dank. Die „Kunst-Insel" des New Yorkers Vito Acconci liegt vor dem barocken Hintergrund der Mariahilferkirche (links) attraktiv vor Anker, in unmittelbarer Nachbarschaft zum Kunsthaus, über zwei filigrane Metallstege (rechts) mit beiden Murufern verbunden. An Bord der Insel befinden sich ein kleines exklusives Café mit spektakulären goldenen Toiletten (unten links) sowie eine kleine Bühne mit Sitzreihen. Abends ist die Insel in geheimnisvolles bläuliches Licht getaucht – sie ist die absolute Attraktion aller Graz-Besucher.

Now Graz also has its own Island in the Mur – thanks to the Cultural Capital 2003. The "ARTificial island" of the New York architect Vito Acconci is attractively anchored in front of the Baroque backdrop of Mariahilfer church (left), in the immediate vicinity of the Kunsthaus, and is connected to both banks via two filigreed metal foot-bridges (right). On board the island, there is a small exclusive café with spectacular, golden toilets (below left), as well as a small stage with rows of seats. In the evening, the island is bathed in mysterious, bluish light – it is the absolute attraction for all visitors to Graz.

Oben: Innenansicht von Richard Kriesches elegantem Lift, der den Besucher in Augenhöhe mit der barocken Madonna am Eisernen Tor brachte.
Above: Interior view of Richard Kriesche's elegant lift on the Eisernes Tor, taking visitors up to eye-level with the Baroque Madonna.

Unten: Die Helmut-List-Halle in der Waagner-Biró-Straße Nr. 98a, ein Aufführungsort der akustischen Perfektion.
Below: The Helmut-List Hall at Waagner-Biró-Strasse No. 98a, an acoustically perfect performance venue.

Rechts und unten: Die Stadthalle für alle im Messegelände in der Conrad-von-Hötzendorf-Straße nach einem Entwurf von Klaus Kada. Besonders markant: das weit vorspringende Dach, das schon von weitem zu sehen ist.
Right and below: The Stadthalle, according to the design of Klaus Kada: the event and congress centre on the trade fair grounds in Conrad-von-Hötzendorf-Strasse. Particularly striking: the protruding roof, which can be seen from far away.

Oben: Die neue Grazer Bahnhofshalle als überdimensionaler Rahmen für Peter Koglers dekorative Illusionsräume in den Farben Schwarz, Rot und Weiß, ebenfalls ein Erbe des Jahres 2003. Sicherlich mit ein Grund, warum der Grazer Bahnhof bereits zum zweiten Mal zum Schönsten Österreichs gewählt wurde.
Above: The new train station hall in Graz is one giant screen for Peter Kogler's decorative illusionary spaces in black, red and white, which is also a legacy of the year 2003. It is certainly one of the reasons why Graz train station has already been elected twice the most beautiful of its kind in Austria.

Rechts: Der schwarze Uhrturmschatten – temporäre Kunst für das Jahr 2003, jetzt schon lange Vergangenheit. Heute ziert er das Shoppingcenter Seiersberg südlich von Graz.
Right: The black shadow of the Clock Tower – temporary art for the year 2003, which is now already a thing of the past. Today it is a highlight in the Seiersberg shopping centre south of Graz.

ANNENHOF
UNIQA
UHR
Canon

Die Vorstadt

Murvorstadt nannte man das freie, unbefestigte Gebiet am rechten Murufer im Westen von Graz, das die heutigen Bezirke Lend und Gries umfasst. Hier wohnten die ärmsten Schichten der Bevölkerung. Und hier befand sich seit dem 13. Jahrhundert ein Bürgerspital, das im Laufe der Zeit durch zahlreiche Schenkungen ausgedehnte Besitzungen erlangte. Auch der Landesfürst hatte hier Ländereien, die er aber aus Geldnot großteils an die Familie der Eggenberger verkaufen musste. Nach diesem steirischen Adelsgeschlecht, das besonders in den Türkenkriegen und im Dreißigjährigen Krieg eine wichtige Rolle spielte, ist heute ein ganzer Stadtbezirk benannt. Dort ließ 1625 Hans Ulrich von Eggenberg als Gubernator von Innerösterreich seinen Familiensitz von Giovanni Pietro de Pomis zu einem fürstlichen Palast ausbauen – Schloss Eggenberg.
Seit dem 16. Jahrhundert wurde das Murufer immer mehr gesichert, so dass sich die Vorstadt weiter ausdehnen konnte. Bereits um 1580 war ein Großteil der Mariahilferstraße (wo wir heute Eisernes Haus und Kunsthaus finden) verbaut. Damals begann auch das Bürgerspital

Links: Das Teleobjektiv macht's möglich – die nächtlich beleuchtete Annenstraße mündet direkt in der Franziskanerkirche und (scheinbar) auch in der weit entfernten Herz-Jesu-Kirche.
Left: A telephoto lens makes it possible – Annenstrasse, lit up at night, flows directly into the Franciscan church and (seemingly) also into the far-away Herz-Jesu church.

seine Gründe zu verkaufen, und rege Bautätigkeit setzte ein. Während des Dreißigjährigen Krieges (1618–1648) siedelten sich hier Flüchtlinge aus allen Teilen des Reiches an. Da wegen der beständigen Türkengefahr 1663 viele Häuser der östlichen Grazer Vorstädte niedergerissen werden mussten, kamen deren Bewohner ebenfalls auf das sichere westliche Murufer. So stieg die Bevölkerungszahl von 3400 im Jahr 1663 auf fast 12.000 im Jahr 1783. Damit hatte man die Innenstadt um fast ein Drittel überflügelt.
Wer waren aber die Bewohner dieser Vorstadt? Sie zählten zu den unteren Schichten, waren unselbstständig und ohne jedes Vermögen. Ihren Unterhalt verdingten sie meist als Bedienstete des Adels und als Taglöhner. Zahlreich waren hier auch Grazer Witwen, die in ihrer Not in die wesentlich günstigere Vorstadt zogen und sich als Wäscherinnen oder Dienstboten über Wasser hielten. Sie lebten alle am Rand des Existenzminimums. Die kleinen Gasthäuser boten Strolchen, Abenteurern und Dirnen Unterschlupf, die Keuschen beherbergten allerlei Gesindel. Verwahrloste Kinder schlossen sich zu Banden zusammen und machten die Murvorstadt gemeinsam mit zahlreichen Räuberbanden zu einer verrufenen und unsicheren Gegend. Doch im Laufe der Zeit entwickelten sich Lend- und Griesplatz zu Straßendorfplätzen an der wichtigen Nord-Süd-Verbindungsstrecke. Denn seit 1728 verlief hier eine Kommerzialstraße von Wien über den Semmering, Graz, Marburg und Laibach zum Adriahafen Triest. Sie gehörte zu einem Straßensystem, das Kaiser Karl VI., der Vater Maria Theresias, in wirtschaftlich und strategisch wichtige Gebiete anlegen ließ. Im Stadtgebiet von Graz führte diese Chaussee über die Wienerstraße, den Lendplatz, die Mariahilferstraße, den Murplatz (heute Südtirolerplatz), die Griesgasse und den Griesplatz in die Triesterstraße.
Aus den alten Vieh- und Getreidemärkten von Lend- und Griesplatz wurden Verkehrsknotenpunkte, deren Treiben vom Frachtfuhrwesen und Militär bestimmt war.
Im Laufe der Zeit entstanden an der Mur zahlreiche Wasserschutzbauten, die den immer wieder über die Ufer tretenden Fluss zähmen sollten. Ganz wild ging es aber am 8. Juni 1827 zu, als die Hochwasser führende Mur die Hauptbrücke wegriss und die gesamte Vorstadt bis zur Pfarrkirche St. Andrä überflutete. Erst die im späten 19. Jahrhundert durchgeführte Murregulierung brachte auf Dauer wirksamen Hochwasserschutz. Nun war Graz auf dem Sprung zur Großstadt. Alles war in urbaner Veränderung, die alten Vorstädte und die 1786 von Caspar Andreas Edler von Jakomini um den nach ihm benannten Platz sternförmig angelegte Vorstadt im Süden wuchsen mit der Altstadt zusammen – das größere Graz entstand.

The Suburbs

The open, unfortified area on the right bank of the Mur in the western part of Graz, which today covers the districts of Lend and Gries, was once called the Murvorstadt (Mur suburbs). This was where the poorest strata of society lived. Since the 13th century, it had also been the location of a citizens' hospital, which over time acquired extensive properties through a number of gifts. The sovereign also had estates there; however, a large part of them had to be sold to the Eggenberg family due to financial difficulties. Today a whole district is named after this Styrian noble house, which played a particularly important role in the Turkish Wars and in

the Thirty Years War. In 1625, Hans Ulrich von Eggenberg, in his function as governor of Inner Austria, commissioned Giovanni Pietro de Pomis with the enlargement of his family residence there into a magnificent palace – Eggenberg Palace. Since the 16th century, the banks of the Mur had been increasingly fortified so that the Vorstadt could continue to spread. As early as in 1580, a major section of Mariahilferstrasse (where the Iron House and the Kunsthaus [House of Art] are located today) was formed by a line of houses. The citizens' hospital also started to sell its plots of land at this time and bustling construction work began. During the Thirty Years War (1618–1648), refugees from all over the empire settled there. Due to the constant danger posed by the Turks, a large number of houses had to be pulled down in the eastern suburbs of Graz in 1663, and their inhabitants moved to the safe west bank of the Mur. Thus, the number of inhabitants increased from 3,400 in 1663 to almost 12,000 in 1783. As a result, the town centre was outstripped by almost a third. But who were the inhabitants of the Vorstadt? They belonged to the lower classes, were economically dependent and without any property. They usually earned their living by working as servants for the nobility and as day-labourers. There was also a large number of widows, who, from sheer need, moved to the much cheaper Vorstadt and kept their heads above water by working as laundrywomen or servants. They all lived on the edge of poverty. The small inns served as hide-outs for ruffians, adventurers, and prostitutes, and the run-down houses accommodated all kinds of riff raff. Neglected children banded together into gangs and together with a number of bands of robbers turned the Murvorstadt into a disreputable and unsafe area. However, over the years, Lendplatz and Griesplatz developed into street village squares along the important North-South route. Since 1728, there had been a commercial route running from Vienna across the Semmering, Graz, Maribor, and Ljubljana, to the Adriatic harbour of Trieste. It was part of a street system that Emperor Karl VI, the father of Maria Theresia, had laid out in economically and strategically important areas. In the town centre of Graz, this road led via Wienerstrasse, Lendplatz, Mariahilferstrasse, the former Murplatz (today's Südtirolerplatz), Griesgasse, and Griesplatz into Triesterstrasse.

The old cattle and grain markets at Lendplatz and Griesplatz became traffic junctions bustling with cargo carriers and the military.

Over the years, a number of protective dams were constructed along the Mur, whose purpose was to tame the river which burst its banks again and again. However, Graz was facing its wildest time, on June 8, 1827, when the Mur, then in flood, tore down the main bridge and flooded the whole Vorstadt, all the way to the St. Andrä parish church. Only the regulation of the Mur, which was carried out in the late 19th century, provided a lasting and effective protection against floods. Now Graz was on its way to becoming a large city. Everything was in urban change: the old suburbs and the suburb in the south, which was laid out by Caspar Andreas Edler von Jakomini in 1786 in the shape of a star around the square named after him, merged with the old part of the city – greater Graz was born.

Rechts: Die Mariahilferstraße zwischen Kunsthaus und Lendplatz – wie Perlen an einer Kette reiht sich hier Lokal an Lokal zu einer einzigen Vergnügungsmeile.

Right: Mariahilferstrasse, between the Kunsthaus and Lendplatz – like pearls on a necklace, there is one bar after the other forming one single amusement mile.

MURGALERIE
BROT & SPIELE
warning! friendly waiters
RUNNERS POINT
Café Baccara
PUNTIGAMER BIER
NIGHT-CLUB
Mariahilferstraße
Heineken

Links oben: Die Kirche der Barmherzigen Brüder in der Annenstraße, ein barocker Bau mit eindrucksvoll geschwungener Fassade, der Anfang des 18. Jahrhunderts von Johann Georg Stengg erbaut wurde.
Above left: The church of the Hospitallers in Annenstrasse, a Baroque building constructed by Johann Georg Stengg at the beginning of the 18th century, featuring an impressively curved façade.

Links Mitte: Bauernmarkt auf dem Lendplatz.
Centre left: Farmers' market on Lendplatz.

Links unten: Blick in das Szenelokal „Pilar" im schlossartigen ehemaligen Renaissancebau Wertl von Wertlsperg (Anfang 17. Jahrhundert) in der Mariahilferstraße, daneben das Schloss- und Schlüsselmuseum der Hans-Schell-Collection in der Wienerstraße 10 (Lendplatz).
Bottom left: View into the trendy "Pilar" bar in the former castle-like Renaissance building "Wertl von Wertlsperg" (beginning of the 17th century) in Mariahilferstrasse. Next to it is the Lock and Key Museum of the Hans-Schell Collection at Wienerstrasse 10 (Lendplatz).

Links: Blick vom Schloßberg auf die alte Vorstadt, die Bezirke Lend und Gries versinken im Schnee – ein eher seltener Anblick in Graz.

Left: View from the Schlossberg of the old suburb. The districts of Lend and Gries sink into the snow – not a very common sight in Graz.

Unten: Die „Nürnberger Häuser" am Lendkai, deren Bauherr Leopold Böhm, der Vater des berühmten Dirigenten Karl Böhm und Großvater des Schauspielers Karlheinz Böhm war.

Below: The "Nuremburg Houses" on Lendkai, commissioned by Leopold Böhm, father of the famous conductor Karl Böhm and grandfather of the actor Karlheinz Böhm.

Unten: Jugendstilmosaik „Der Frühling“ des Koloman-Moser-Schülers Leopold Forstner im Grandhotel Wiesler.
Below: The Art Nouveau mosaic “Spring” by Leopold Forstner, a pupil of Koloman Moser, in the Wiesler Grand Hotel.

Rechts: Die 2002 restaurierte Kreuzigungsgruppe auf dem Kalvarienberg. Unter Führung der Jesuiten wurden zwischen 1656 und 1660 die einzelnen Kalvarienbergstationen erstellt.
Right: Renovated in 2002, the crucifixion group on the Calvary. The Jesuits were the driving force behind the setting-up of the individual Calvary stations between 1656 and 1660.

Rechts: Stimmungsbilder aus der alten Gries-Vorstadt – am Beginn der Griesgasse finden wir seit dem 17. Jahrhundert nahezu unverändert die Bäckerei „Zum Griesbäcker“, nur ein Stück weiter auf dem Griesplatz Nummer 34 steht ein 1663 erbautes Backhaus, das 1982 restauriert wurde und heute den Schnitzelwirt „Zu den drei goldenen Kugeln“ beherbergt.
Right: Impressions of the old Gries suburb – at the beginning of Griesgasse, one can still find the bakery “Zum Griesbäcker”, nearly unchanged since the 17th century; and only a little bit further, at Griesplatz No. 34, there is another bakery dating from 1663, which was restored in 1982 and now houses the schnitzel restaurant “Zu den drei goldenen Kugeln”.

Links: Die 1999 neu errichtete Synagoge: Mit Originalziegeln des 1938 in der „Reichskristallnacht" niedergebrannten Gebäudes wurde an derselben Stelle am Murufer an der Augartenbrücke auch ein Stück des Vorgängerbaus wieder errichtet.
Left: The synagogue, rebuilt in 1999: Using the original bricks of the building that burned down in the "Night of Broken Glass" in 1938, a piece of the original building now rests on the exactly the same spot on the bank next to the Augarten bridge.

Mitte: Das „Museum der Wahrnehmung" (MUWA) am Augarten. Ein Ort der unterschiedlichsten Welten – „oben" das kleine Museum, das sich mit dem Phänomen der Wahrnehmung befasst, „unten" im Keller des achteckigen „Tröpferlbades" von 1903 eine öffentliche Badeanstalt mit Wannen- und Brausebad, aber auch mit „Samadhi", dem schwerelosen Badeerlebnis.
Centre: The "Museum of Perception" (MUWA) in the Augarten park. A place of the most diverse worlds – on the ground floor, there is the small museum which deals with the phenomenon of perception, and in the basement, there is the octagonal "droplet bath" dating from 1903, a public bathing facility with tubs and showers, as well as the "Samadhi" bath offering a weightless bathing experience.

Unten: Das 2003 eröffnete „Kindermuseum" im Augarten, das zum interaktiven Spielen einlädt, daneben der 74 Meter lange „Augartensteg", der den Bezirk Gries mit dem Augarten verbindet.
Below: The "Children's Museum", which was opened in the Augarten park in 2003, invites everybody to interactive games. Next to it, the 74-metre long "Augarten foot-bridge" that connects the Gries district to the Augarten park.

In die neue Vorstadt von heute: Über den idyllischen Hilmteich (links unten) zur Basilika von Mariatrost, einer der größten Barockkirchen der Steiermark.

Into today's new suburb: From idyllic Hilmteich lake (bottom left) to Mariatrost Basilica, one of Styria's largest Baroque churches.

Blick in das Kuppelgewölbe mit den Fresken des kaiserlichen Hofmalers Lukas von Schram, 1733/1741 (unten), und auf das Orgelgehäuse (links).

View into the vaults of the cupola, featuring the frescoes of the imperial court painter Lukas von Schram, 1733/1741 (below), and of the organ casing (left).

Eine Stiege mit 215 Stufen führt zur berühmten Wallfahrtskirche von Mariatrost mit ihren markanten Doppeltürmen. Ab 1709 entstand der Kirchenbau gemeinsam mit einem Kloster des Paulinerordens. Den Hochaltar dominiert die aus dem Stift Rein stammende gotische Madonna von 1465, der wundertätige Kräfte nachgesagt werden.
A staircase with 215 steps leads to the famous Mariatrost pilgrimage church with its distinctive double towers. Starting in 1709, both the church and the monastery of the Paulinian order were built. The high altar is dominated by the Gothic Madonna from the Rein monastery. The Madonna dates back to 1465 and is said to have miraculous powers.

Seit Sommer 2010 ist auch das Schloß Eggenberg Weltkulturerbe – der 1625 nach den Plänen Pietro de Pomis' umgebaute Familiensitz derer von Eggenberg beeindruckt durch die gewaltige barocke Größe ebenso wie durch die Zahlenspielerei des Reichsfürsten Johann Ulrich von Eggenberg. Denn das ganze Gebäude entspricht der Zahlenallegorik des neu eingeführten Gregorianischen Kalenders: 365 Fenster, 31 Räume in jedem Stockwerk, 24 Prunkräume mit 52 Fenstern und Türen. Die vier Ecktürme entsprechen den vier Jahreszeiten.

Surrounded by a park that stands under the protection of the order for the preservation of historical monuments, the family seat of the Eggenberg family, reconstructed in 1625 according to the plans of Pietro de Pomis, not only is impressive due to its enormous Baroque size, but also due to the fascination with numbers of Prince Johann Ulrich von Eggenberg. The whole palace corresponds to the allegory of numbers of the newly introduced Gregorian calendar: 365 windows, 31 rooms on each storey, 24 splendid rooms with 52 windows and doors. The four angle towers correspond to the four seasons.

Über dem mächtigen Hauptportal an der Ostseite des Schlosses, das von einem breiten Graben umgeben ist, prangt das siebenteilige Wappen der Eggenberger mit den drei Raben im Zentrum, die eine Krone tragen.
Above the mighty main portal on the east side of the palace, which is surrounded by a wide moat, the Eggenbergs' seven-piece coat of arms is prominently displayed, featuring the three crown-wearing ravens in the centre.

Rechts: Die im 18. Jahrhundert vorherrschende China-Mode hielt auch hier Einzug, und so wurden drei Prunkräume „indianisch", also ostasiatisch, eingerichtet. Raum 18 wurde als „Cabinett mit chinesischer Spälier" bezeichnet, ist aber in Wahrheit japanisch. Seine Wanddekoration besteht aus einem in acht Streifen geschnittenen Wandschirm.
Right: Chinese fashion, which was prominent in the 18th century, also made its way into the palace and thus three splendid rooms were decorated and furnished in "Indian", i. e. East Asian, style. Room 18 was called the "cabinet with a Chinese wall covering", but in truth, it was Japanese. This wall decoration was made up of a folding screen cut into eight strips.

Ganz oben: Künstlerischer Höhepunkt des Schlosses und des symbolischen Bildprogramms ist der zentrale Planetensaal, in dem sich im Gemäldezyklus des fürstlichen Hofmalers Hans Adam Weissenkirchner Planeten, Elemente, Sternbilder und der gesamte Tierkreis im Auftrag von Johann Seyfried von Eggenberg (1678) zur Verherrlichung der fürstlichen Familie vereinen.
Far top: The artistic highlight of the palace and its symbolic programme of paintings is the centrally located Planet Hall with its cycle of paintings commissioned by Johann Seyfried von Eggenberg (1678). In this cycle, court painter Hans Adam Weissenkirchner unified the planets, elements, constellations, and the whole zodiac and thus paid homage to the House of Eggenberg.

Rechts: Schlafzimmer in der Beletage des Schlosses, in dessen Himmelbett 1765 Maria Theresia (höchstwahrscheinlich) ruhte.
Right: Bedroom on the first floor of the palace, where Maria Theresia is said to have (very probably) rested in the four-poster bed in 1765.

Oben: Die Ruine Gösting im Norden von Graz. Bereits 1045 erstmals erwähnt, befand sich die Burg bis 1622 im Besitz des Landesfürsten. Da die Stadt Graz in ihren Mauern Schießpulver aufbewahrte, setzte ein Blitzschlag im Jahr 1723 die Burg in Flammen und machte sie zur Ruine. Heute befindet sie sich in Privatbesitz, ihren teilweisen Wiederaufbau verdankt die Burg dem sehr aktiven Burgverein.
Above: The Gösting castle ruins to the north of Graz. Mentioned for the first time as early as in 1045, the castle was in the possession of the sovereign up to 1622. Since the City of Graz used to store gunpowder within its walls, a bolt of lightning set the castle on fire in 1723 and reduced it to ruins. Today the castle is privately owned and owes its partial reconstruction to the very active "Burgverein" association.

Links: Blick vom Jungfernsprung, einem steilen Felsen neben der Ruine, Richtung Norden ins Murtal.
Left: Looking north into the Mur valley from the so-called "Virgin's Leap", a steep cliff next to the ruins.

Rechts: Schloss Gösting am Fuß des Burgberges direkt an der Durchzugsstraße ist einer der reizvollsten Barockbauten des Landes, 1728 im Auftrag von Ignaz Maria Attems fertig gestellt und von zwei hübschen Eckpavillons umgeben.
Right: Gösting Palace, situated at the foot of the castle hill directly at the thoroughfare, is one of the province's most charming Baroque buildings. It was commissioned by Ignaz Maria Attems, finished in 1728, and is surrounded by two beautiful corner pavilions.

Mitte: Weizenfeld im Süden von Graz, daneben der romantische Thalersee, wo der berühmteste Sohn der Gemeinde Thal, Arnold Schwarzenegger, um die Hand seiner Maria Shriver anhielt.
Centre: Wheatfield to the south of Graz. Next to it, the romantic Thalersee lake, where the most famous son of the municipality of Thal, Arnold Schwarzenegger, asked for the hand of Maria Shriver.

Unten: Der Skulpturenpark in Unterpremstätten im Gelände des Schwarzl-Freizeitzentrums zeigt an die 60 Objekte von Künstlern wie Fritz Wotruba, Hans Kupelwieser und Erwin Wurm. Daneben die Kirche Zum heiligen Jakob in Thal in der farbenfrohen fantastischen Erweiterung durch den Wiener Künstler Ernst Fuchs (1987).
Below: The sculpture park in Unterpremstätten on the grounds of the Schwarzl-Recreation-Centre displays about 60 works of art by artists, such as Fritz Wotruba, Hans Kupelwieser, and Erwin Wurm. On the right, St. Jacob's church in Thal with its colourful, fantastic extension according to the plans of the Viennese artist Ernst Fuchs (1987).

Graz im historischen Überblick

4000 v. Chr. Früheste Besiedlung (Schloßberg, Karmeliterplatz)
Seit dem 2. Jahrhundert v. Chr. Teil des keltischen Königreiches Noricum
15 v. Chr. bis 476 n. Chr. gehört das Gebiet zum Römischen Reich. Von einer am Westrand des Grazer Beckens Nord-Süd verlaufenden Römerstraße zweigt ein Weg nach Osten ab, der die Mur über eine Furt bei der heutigen Hauptbrücke überquert und entlang der Sporgasse über die alten Siedlungsgebiete am Karmeliterplatz Richtung Ungarn führt
Im 6. Jahrhundert wandern nach Völkerwanderungszeit, Hunnensturm und Untergang des Weströmischen Reiches slawische Stämme in das verödete Gebiet und errichten auf dem Schloßberg eine kleine Burg (slaw. gradec), von der sich der Name Graz ableitet.
Ende des 8. Jahrhunderts schlägt Karl der Große die Awaren, die bayrische Besiedlung des Raumes beginnt
955 besiegt Kaiser Otto I. auf dem Lechfeld die Ungarn, die nun wieder nach Osten zurückgedrängt werden. Zur Sicherung des Reiches entsteht ein Markengürtel vor den Ostalpen. Die Karantanische Mark wird zur Keimzelle der Steiermark
1128 erste Erwähnung von Graz in einer Urkunde des Klosters Rein, neueste Forschungen datieren eine erste Erwähnung bereits auf 1091
Um 1160 übernimmt der Traungauer Markgraf Otakar III. von Steyr das Grazer Gebiet
1164 Nennung eines Marktes, Graz entwickelt sich zur Landeshauptstadt
1180 wird die Steiermark von Kaiser Friedrich Barbarossa zum Herzogtum erhoben und von Bayern unabhängig
1240/45 erhält Graz den Panther des steirischen Herzogs als Stadtsiegel
1379 Nach der Teilung des Habsburgerreiches im Vertrag von Neuberg wird die Stadt zur Residenz der Leopoldinischen Linie und damit zum Zentrum von Innerösterreich
1435 bis 1493 erlebt Graz seine erste Blüte: Herzog Friedrich V. (ab 1440 als Friedrich III. deutscher König, ab 1452 römischer Kaiser) macht die Stadt zu seiner bevorzugten Residenz, errichtet eine Stadtburg und lässt die alte Pfarrkirche Zum heiligen Ägydius im gotischen Stil neu errichten (heute Dom)
1439 und 1495 Vertreibung der Juden
1480 Türken, Pest und Heuschrecken suchen den Grazer Raum heim
1499 Kaiser Maximilian I., Friedrichs Sohn, lässt in der Burg eine gotische Doppelwendeltreppe errichten
Ab 1544 wird Graz nach Erlass Kaiser Ferdinands I. durch Domenico dell'Aglio zur Hauptfestung Innerösterreichs ausgebaut
1564 bis 1619 zweite Blüte der Stadt: Graz wird Erzherzog Karls Residenzstadt von Innerösterreich
1570 Errichtung der evangelischen Stiftskirche und -schule (heute Paradeishof, mit Johannes Kepler als Lehrer von 1594 bis 1600)
1572 Berufung der Jesuiten nach Graz, die Rekatholisierung beginnt

1600 Ausweisung aller evangelischen Bürger
1619 Erzherzog Ferdinand wird zum römischen Kaiser gewählt und zieht mit seinem Hof nach Wien
1642 Antonio Solar erbaut das Landeszeughaus
1673 Kaiser Leopold I. vermählt sich in Graz mit Erzherzogin Claudia Felicitas von Tirol
1664 Nach den Türkensiegen verliert Graz seine Bedeutung als Zentrum der Verteidigung
1773 Der Jesuitenorden wird vom Papst aufgelöst, die Grazer Universität vom Staat übernommen
1782 Die Auflassung der alten Stadtbefestigungen wird verfügt
1786 Graz wird Bischofssitz
1797 Die französische Revolutionsarmee Napoleons rückt in Graz ein
1809 Nach erfolgloser dreiwöchiger Belagerung des Schloßbergs verlangt Napoleon im Friedensvertrag von Schönbrunn die Schleifung der Festung. Nur Uhrturm und Glocken-turm bleiben für ein hohes Lösegeld
1811 Erzherzog Johann gründet mit seinen Sammlungen das Joanneum
19. Jahrhundert Graz wird zur Gartenstadt, der Schloßberg zur öffentlichen Parkanlage, das alte Glacis zum Stadtpark (1868), Volksgarten und Augarten entstehen, Hilm-teich und Leechwald werden erworben. Universitäten, Rathaus, Opernhaus und Prestigebauten werden errichtet
1899 Eine elektrische Straßenbahn ersetzt die Pferdebahn
1919 Graz verliert nach dem Ersten Weltkrieg sein Hinterland im Süden und gerät in eine Randlage
1938 Durch Eingemeindung wächst die Stadt von sechs auf 16 (heute 17) Bezirke
1944/45 Schwere Luftangriffe: 9 % der Gebäude werden völlig zerstört, 36 % beschädigt. Ein Stollensystem im Schloßberg dient als Luftschutzkeller
April 1945 Sowjetische Truppen besetzen Graz und werden im Juli von den Engländern abgelöst
1960 Gründung des „Forum Stadtpark", Aufstieg von Graz zu einem Zentrum der künstlerischen Avantgarde im deutschen Sprachraum
1968 Erster „steirischer herbst"
1974 Die Aktion „Rettet die Grazer Altstadt" verhindert eine Tiefgarage unter dem Landhaushof und führt zum Beschluss des Grazer Altstadterhaltungsgesetzes
1978 850-Jahr-Feier der Stadt
1999 Grazer Altstadt wird in die Liste des Weltkulturerbes aufgenommen
2003 Graz Kulturhauptstadt Europas
2005 Graz und ganz Österreich im Jubiläumsjahr: 60 Jahre Ende Zweiter Weltkrieg und Zweite Republik, 50 Jahre Staatsvertrag, zehn Jahre EU
2010 Schloß Eggenberg wird Unesco-Weltkulturerbe

Links: Der Hauptplatz gegen Norden mit Schloßberg. Aquarellierte Federzeichnung von Ferdinand Runk, 1795.
Left: Hauptplatz to the north with the Schlossberg. Water-coloured pen-and-ink drawing by Ferdinand Runk, 1795.

A historical overview of Graz

4000 BC Earliest settlement (Schlossberg, Karmeliterplatz)
Since the 2nd century BC part of the Celtic kingdom Noricum
15 BC to 467 AD The territory belonged to the Roman Empire. Branching off from the Roman road running north to south along the western edge of the Graz Basin was a road to the East, which crossed the Mur via a fort and led to Hungary along Sporgasse and through the old settlement areas on Karmeliterplatz
In the 6th century, following the migration of peoples, the attack of the Huns, and the fall of the West Roman Empire, Slavic tribes migrated into the deserted land and built a small castle (Slavic gradec), from which the name Graz stems, on the Schlossberg.
At the end of the 8th century, Charlemagne defeated the Avars; the Bavarian settlement of this area began
955 Emperor Otto I defeated the Hungarians on the Lechfeld and drove them back again to the East. A belt of marches was created in front of the Eastern Alps in order to protect the empire. The Carantanian March became the nucleus of Styria
1128 Graz was first mentioned in a document of the Rein monastery, and the latest state of research dates its first documentary mention back to as early as 1091
Around 1160 Traungau Margrave Otakar III von Steyr took over the area of Graz
1164 Graz became a market and then was well on its way to becoming the capital
1180 Emperor Friedrich Barbarossa elevated Styria to a duchy and thus made it independent of Bavaria
1240/45 Graz was given the panther of the Styrian duke as its town seal
1379 After the division of the Habsburg Empire in the Treaty of Neuberg, the town became the residence of the Leopoldinian line and thus the centre of Inner Austria
From 1435 to 1493 Graz experienced its first heydays: Duke Friedrich V (from 1440 on, Friedrich III, the German King, and from 1452 on, the Roman Emperor) made the town his most favourite residence, built a town castle and had the old St. Ägydius parish church rebuilt in Gothic style (today's cathedral)
1439 and 1495 Expulsion of the Jews
In 1480 the Turks, the plague and locusts struck the area of Graz
In 1499 Emperor Maximilian I, Friedrich's son, had a Gothic double spiral staircase built in the castle
Starting in 1544 Domenico dell'Aglio built Graz up into the main fortress of Inner Austria by decree of Emperor Ferdinand I
From 1564 to 1619 the second heydays of the town: Graz became Archduke Karl's residential capital of Inner Austria
1570 Founding of the Protestant collegiate church and school (today's Paradeishof, where Johannes Kepler taught from 1594 to 1600)

1572 Appointment of the Jesuits to Graz, and the Catholic Renewal began
1600 Banishment of all Protestant citizens
1619 Archduke Ferdinand was crowned Roman Emperor and he and his court moved to Vienna
1642 Antonio Solar built the Landeszeughaus (Provincial Armoury)
1673 Emperor Leopold I married Archduchess Claudia Felicitas von Tirol in Graz
1664 After the victories over the Turks, Graz lost its importance as a centre of defence
1773 The order of the Jesuits was dissolved by the pope; the university in Graz was taken over by the state
1782 The town's old fortifications were abandoned
1786 Graz became the seat of the bishop
1797 Napoleon's French revolutionary army marched into Graz
1809 After an unsuccessful three week long siege of the Schlossberg, Napoleon demanded the razing of the fortress in the Peace Treaty of Schönbrunn. Only the clock tower and the bell tower were saved after the payment of a high ransom
1811 Archduke Johann founded the Joanneum with his collections
19th century Graz turned into the garden city, the Schlossberg into a public park facility, the old Glacis into the City Park (1868); the Volksgarten and the Augarten parks were laid out, and lake Hilmteich and the Leechwald forests were purchased. The universities, the city hall, the opera house and prestigious buildings were constructed
1899 An electric tram replaced the horse-drawn tram
1919 After World War I, Graz lost its land to the South and was pushed into a marginal position
1938 By the incorporation of the surrounding villages, the city increased from 6 to 16 (today 17) districts
1944/45 Heavy air raids: 9 % of the buildings were completely destroyed, and 36 % were damaged. A tunnel system in the Schlossberg was used as an air-raid shelter
April of 1945 Soviet troops occupied Graz; they were replaced by the English in July
1960 Founding of the Forum Stadtpark, and the rise of Graz to a centre of the artistic avant-garde in the German-speaking area
1968 The first steirischer herbst
1974 The campaign "Save Graz's historic centre" averted an underground car park beneath the Landhaus courtyard and led to the passing of the Act for the Preservation of the Historical Centre of Graz

1978 The city celebrated its 850th anniversary
1999 The historic centre of Graz was added to the UNESCO World Cultural Heritage list
2003 Graz, the Cultural Capital of Europe
2005 Graz and the whole of Austria celebrate the jubilee year: 60th anniversary of the end of World War II and the beginning of the Second Republic, 50th anniversary of the Austrian State; Treaty, 10 years of EU membership
2010 Schloss Eggenberg was added to the UNESCO World Cultural Heritage list